Teaching Pal 2

Authors and Advisors

Alma Flor Ada • Kylene Beers • F. Isabel Campoy
Joyce Armstrong Carroll • Nathan Clemens
Anne Cunningham • Martha C. Hougen
Elena Izquierdo • Carol Jago • Erik Palmer
Robert E. Probst • Shane Templeton • Julie Washington

Contributing Consultants

David Dockterman • Mindset Works®
Jill Eggleton

Printed in the U.S.A.

ISBN 978-1-328-51717-3

4 5 6 7 8 9 10 0868 27 26 25 24 23 22 21 20 19

4500757645 B C D E F G

Navigating the Teaching Pal

The Teaching Pal is a companion to the Teacher's Guide, providing point-of-use instructional notes for using the student texts in *my*Book for different purposes.

Blue Notes
READ FOR UNDERSTANDING

During a first reading of the complete text, use these notes to guide collaborative discussion about the gist of the text.

READ FOR UNDERSTANDING

ASK: How do you know that Clark's plan is working? Find evidence in the text and picture that helps you answer the question. *(The picture shows that everyone still has his or her own lunch, so Clark has not eaten them. The words "Way to go!" show that his friends are proud of how Clark is acting. Clark says that "Lunch is fun." Clark must be feeling good about how his plan is working out.)*

DOK 2

Purple Notes
TARGETED CLOSE READ

During subsequent readings, use these notes to take a closer look at sections of the text to apply a reading skill.

TARGETED CLOSE READ

Setting

Have children reread pages 24–26 to analyze the setting.

ASK: Where do events in the story take place? *(at school: the playground, the lunchroom, the classroom)*

ANNOTATION TIP: Have children circle phrases that help them know where the events on each page are taking place. *("In class"; "At lunch"; "At playtime")*

FOLLOW-UP: Why are the changes to the setting important? *(The changes show how Clark acts in different places around the school and how he disrupts things.)*

DOK 3

Yellow Notes

Use these notes for teaching support on the pages that appear before and after each text.

Academic Discussion

Use the TURN AND TALK routine. Remind children to follow agreed-upon discussion rules.

Possible responses:

1. *I asked myself, "How is Clark going to learn to follow the rules?" Asking questions helps me remember the details in the story.* DOK 2
2. *Clark's friends won't play with him because he is too wild. Clark is sad. He looks sad in the illustration, and then he talks to his teacher about what to do.* DOK 2
3. *One of Clark's rules is, "Only munch your own lunch." Following that rule helps Clark be a good citizen because he is not eating food that does not belong to him.* DOK 3

Red Notes
NOTICE & NOTE

Use these notes to help children learn to look for signposts in a text in order to create meaning.

Notice & Note

Words of the Wiser

Remind children that the main character of a story often gets help or advice from another character who is older and wiser. When this happens, they should stop to notice and note.

Have children explain why they might use this strategy on page 21. *(Mrs. Inkydink gives Clark good advice. She tells Clark that he does things too hard, and "there's a time and place for everything.")*

Remind them of the Anchor Question: **What's the life lesson and how might it affect Clark?** *(The life lesson is that there is a time and place for everything. Clark might listen to her words and control his behavior.)*

DOK 3

TABLE OF CONTENTS

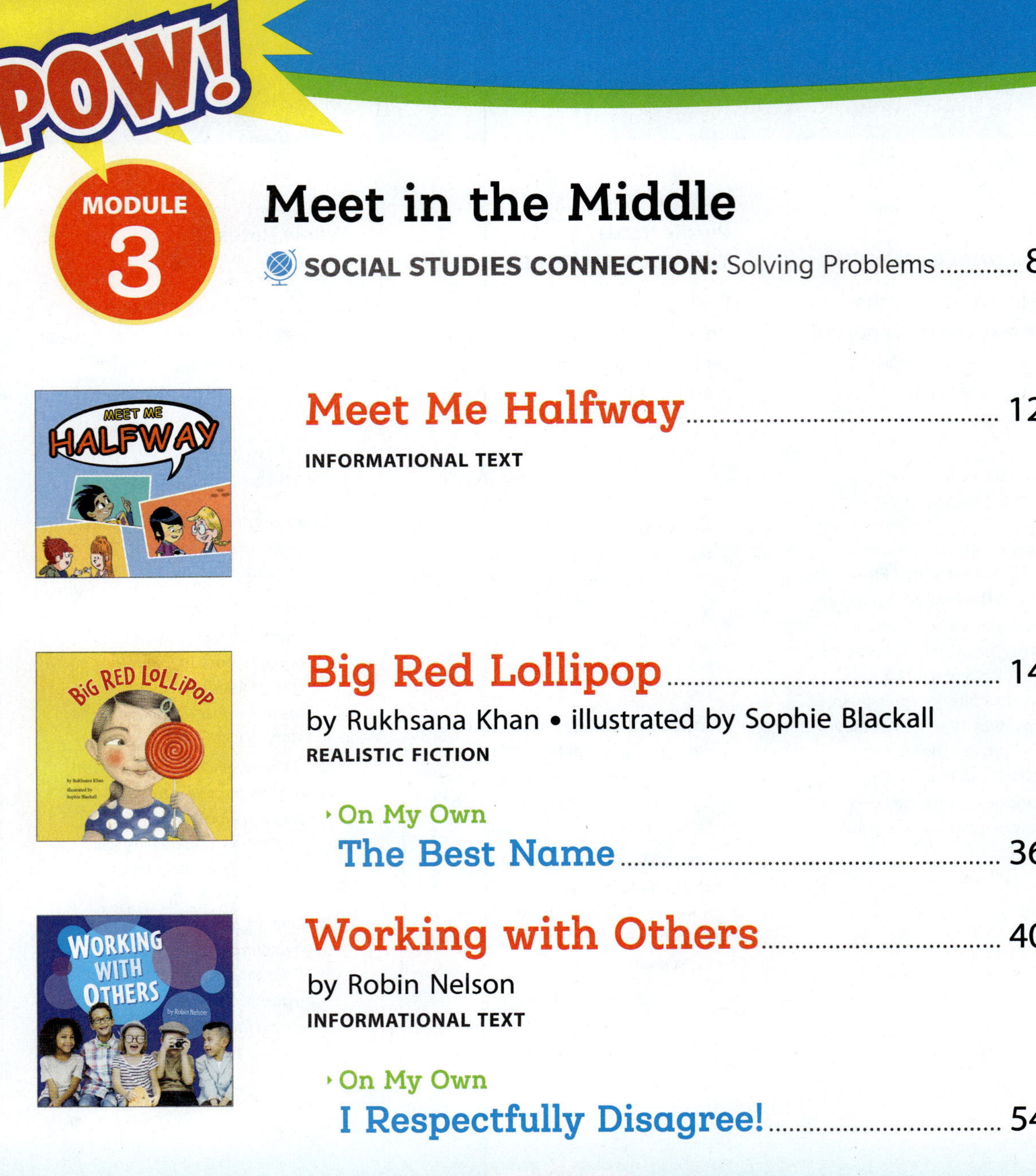

Meet in the Middle

4

5

MODULE 4

Once Upon a Time

7

MODULE 3

Meet in the Middle

"You must speak words that matter."

—Kate DiCamillo

Introduce the Topic

- **Read aloud** the module title, *Meet in the Middle.*
- **Tell children** that in this module they will be reading texts about solving problems.
- **Have children** share prior knowledge about the topic or word associations for solving problems. Record their ideas in a web.

Discuss the Quotation

- **Read aloud** the quotation by Kate DiCamillo.
- **Lead a discussion** in which children try to explain the quote in their own words. Explain the meaning, as needed: *We need to pay attention to what we say, because our words can have powerful effects.*

ASK: Describe a time when something you said had an effect on another person. *(Accept reasonable responses.)*

8

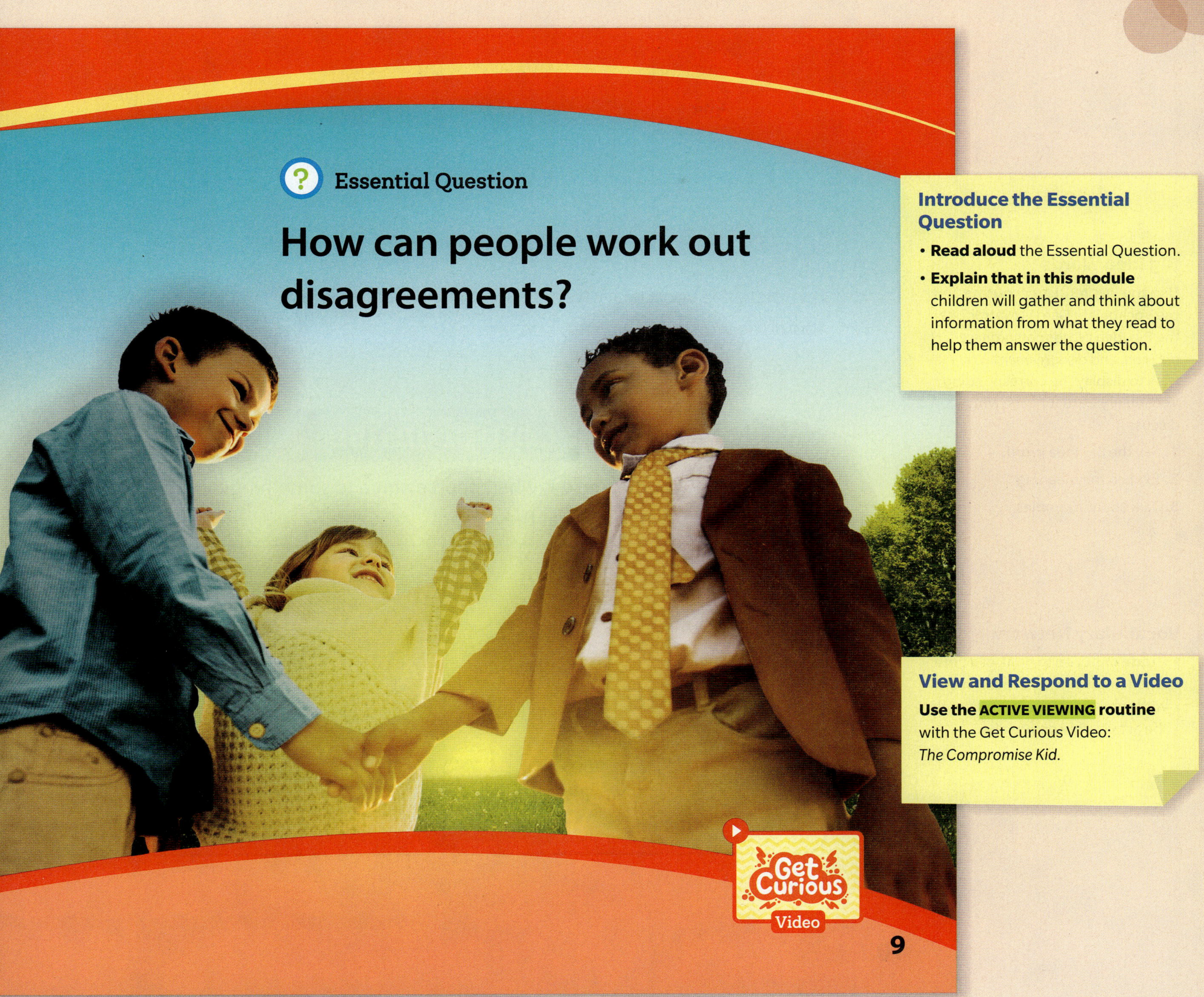

Introduce the Essential Question

- **Read aloud** the Essential Question.
- **Explain that in this module** children will gather and think about information from what they read to help them answer the question.

View and Respond to a Video

Use the ACTIVE VIEWING routine with the Get Curious Video: *The Compromise Kid.*

Big Idea Words

Use the VOCABULARY routine and the Vocabulary Cards to introduce the Big Idea Words *compromise, decision,* and *disagreement*. You may wish to display the corresponding Vocabulary Card for each word as you discuss it.

1. Say the Big Idea Word.
2. Explain the meaning.
3. Talk about examples.

Vocabulary Network

- **Guide children** to think of a time when they came to an agreement with someone else as they complete the activity for *compromise.*

Big Idea Words

Words About Solving Problems

Complete the Vocabulary Network to show what you know about the words.

compromise

Meaning: A **compromise** is when people agree to something by each giving up a little of what they want.

Synonyms and Antonyms	Drawing

decision

Meaning: When you make a **decision**, you make up your mind about something.

Synonyms and Antonyms	Drawing

disagreement

Meaning: In a **disagreement**, people have different ideas about things.

Synonyms and Antonyms	Drawing

Vocabulary Network

- **Help children** recognize decisions they make every day, such as choosing which clothes to wear in the morning or which games to play at recess.
- **As children complete** the activity for *disagreement,* have them think about how two people might feel if they had different ideas about something important.

READ FOR UNDERSTANDING

Introduce the Text

Read aloud the title, *Meet Me Halfway*. Tell children that it is informational text. Ask them to recall what they know about informational text. *(They give real information about a topic.)*

- Guide children to **set a purpose.**
- **Read the text** with children.

DOK 2

READ FOR UNDERSTANDING

Central Idea

ASK: What is the topic of this text? *(compromise)* **What evidence gives you a clue?** *(The text at the beginning tells what a compromise is. The cartoons give examples of compromises people might make.)*

FOLLOW-UP: How did the people in the first cartoon compromise? *(Each person wanted to hold the dog's leash. They decided to take turns.)* **What was the result?** *(They solved their difference and did not fight about it.)*

DOK 2

Short Read

MEET ME HALFWAY

What does it mean when people say, "Let's meet in the middle"? They are talking about **compromise**, or a way to end a disagreement.

When people compromise, they each give up a little of what they want. These comic strips show examples of compromise.

12

READ FOR UNDERSTANDING

Central Idea

ASK: How did Mario and his mom compromise? Use evidence to explain. *(Mario agreed to clean his room. His mom agreed to let him finish the chapter of the book he was reading before he did so.)* **What evidence tells you their compromise was successful?** *(Mario and his mom did not argue. In the end, they were both happy with the compromise.)*

FOLLOW-UP: What is the central idea of the text on these two pages? *(Knowing how to compromise can help people solve their differences without arguing.)*

DOK 2

 **READ FOR UNDERSTANDING**

Introduce the Text

- **Read aloud** and discuss the information about the genre.
- **Guide children** to set a purpose for reading to monitor what they have read and pause to ask questions to clarify anything that is confusing.
- **Provide information** about the author, Rukhsana Khan.
- **Tell children** to look for and think about the Power Words as they read.

Guided Practice

Prepare to Read

GENRE STUDY **Realistic fiction** stories are made up but could happen in real life. As you read *Big Red Lollipop,* look for:

- characters who act and talk like real people
- a lesson the main character learns
- problems that real people might have

SET A PURPOSE As you read, stop and think if you don't understand something. Reread, ask yourself questions, use what you already know, and look for visual clues to help you understand the text.

POWER WORDS

- invited
- screams
- plead
- musical
- shove
- scoots
- greedy
- scurries

Meet Rukhsana Khan.

14

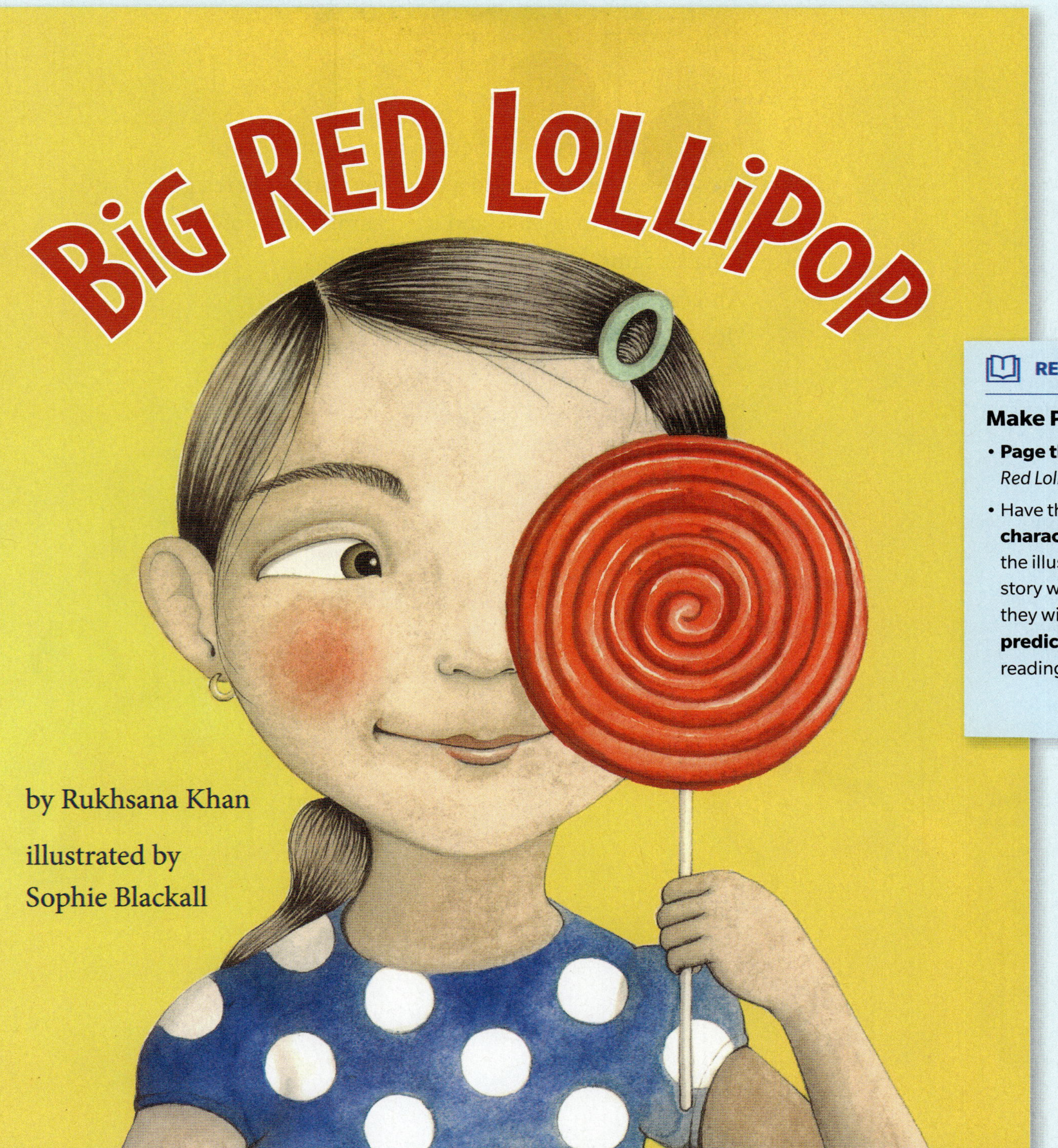

READ FOR UNDERSTANDING

Make Predictions

- **Page through** the beginning of *Big Red Lollipop* with children.
- Have them **use prior knowledge, characteristics of the genre,** and the illustrations to predict what the story will be about. Tell children they will **return to their predictions** after they finish reading the story.

DOK 2

TARGETED CLOSE READ

Point of View

Have children reread pages 16–18 to determine the story's point of view.

ANNOTATION TIP: Have children circle the character who has been invited to the birthday party.

ASK: Who is telling the story? *(Rubina, the character who has been invited to the party)* **What clue in the first sentence on page 16 helps you know?** *(The person telling the story uses the word I.)*

FOLLOW-UP: What thoughts and feelings has Rubina shared with the reader? *(She's excited about the party but doesn't want to take her younger sister; she does what her mother wants even though she doesn't want to; she's worried about what her friend thinks.)*

DOK 2

READ FOR UNDERSTANDING

ASK: Who is Ami? What clues help you figure this out? *(Ami is the mother of the girl who wants to go to the party. The illustration shows the woman with younger children. The girl asks Ami if she can go to the party.)*

DOK 2

I'm so excited I run all the way home from school.

"Ami! I've been invited to a birthday party! There's going to be games and toys, cake and ice cream! Can I go?"

Sana screams, "I wanna go too!"

Ami says, "What's a birthday party?"

"It's when they celebrate the day they were born."

"Why do they do *that*?"

"They just do! Can I go?"

16

Sana screams, "I wanna go too!"

"I can't take *her*! She's not invited."

"Why not?" says Ami.

"They don't do that here!"

Ami says, "Well that's not fair. You call up your friend and ask if you can bring Sana, or else you can't go."

"But Ami! They'll laugh at me! They'll never invite me to another party again!"

Sana screams, "I wanna go too!"

17

READ FOR UNDERSTANDING

Monitor and Clarify

MODEL MONITORING AND CLARIFYING

THINK ALOUD *I'm confused about why Ami insists that her daughter call up her friend and ask if she can bring Sana, so I will reread the text. Ami asked why her daughter can't take Sana. That tells me that she doesn't understand how birthday party invitations work. I still don't understand why she doesn't know this. Then I noticed that the daughter says, "They don't do that here!" That detail helps me answer my question. I think Ami has not lived in America all her life. It may be that it was okay to bring family members to parties where she used to live.*

DOK 2

I say, "Look, Sana, one day you'll get invited to your own friends' parties. Wouldn't you like that better?"

"No! I wanna go now!"

READ FOR UNDERSTANDING

ASK: Why does the main character feel like she has no choice but to call her friend? Look for details in the text. *(The main character has done everything she can do. First she spoke to Sana about wanting to go to one of her friend's parties. Then she begged and pleaded with her mother, but Ami wouldn't listen.)*

FOLLOW-UP: How do you think the main character feels after the call? Explain. *(She's upset. Even though her friend said it was okay to bring her sister, she can tell by the sound of her voice that it really wasn't.)*

DOK 3

I beg and plead, but Ami won't listen. I have no choice. I have to call. Sally says, "All right." But it doesn't sound all right. I know she thinks I'm weird.

18

READ FOR UNDERSTANDING

Phonics/Decoding in Context

Remind children that when a word ends in a final consonant blend, both sounds can be heard at the end of the word. Then have children point to the word *during* and identify the consonants that make up the final blend. **Model blending** the sounds to demonstrate how each sound can be heard. Then have children blend and say the word with you.

TARGETED CLOSE READ

Point of View

Have children reread pages 20–23 to analyze the story's point of view.

ANNOTATION TIP: Have children circle the pronouns that remind them who is telling the story.

ASK: Who is telling the story now? Is that the same or different as before? *(Rubina is still telling the story. It hasn't changed.)*

FOLLOW-UP: What words did you circle that show Rubina is telling the story? (I, mine, me, my, I'm)

DOK 3

READ FOR UNDERSTANDING

Quick Teach Words

As needed to support comprehension, briefly explain the meaning of *ruby* in this context.

- A ring with a *ruby* has a dark red stone.

Before we leave the party, Sally's mom gives us little bags. Inside there are chocolates and candies, a whistle, a ruby ring, and a big red lollipop! Sana eats her big red lollipop on the way home in the car. I save mine for later.

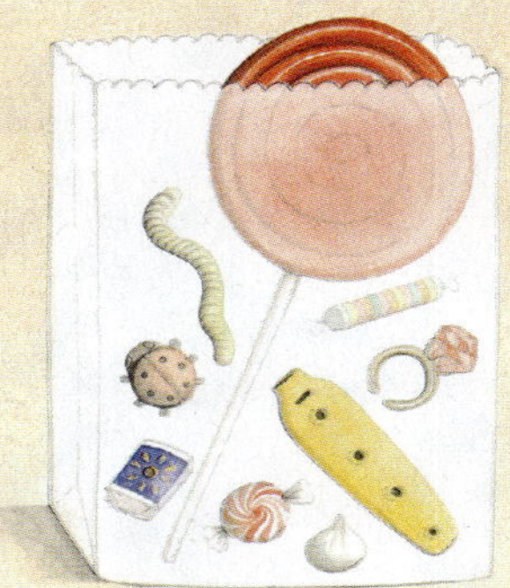

20

Sana doesn't know how to make things last. By bedtime, her candies are all gone, her whistle is broken, and the ruby in her ring is missing. I put my big red lollipop on the top shelf of the fridge to have in the morning.

All night I dream about how good it will taste.

21

READ FOR UNDERSTANDING

ASK: What do you think will happen next? Explain. *(Possible response: The next morning Sana will ask her sister if she will share her lollipop.)*

ASK: How is Rubina different from her younger sister, Sana? *(Rubina wants to save her treats from the party and puts her lollipop away, but Sana eats everything right away and the toys are broken.)*

DOK 2

READ FOR UNDERSTANDING

ASK: How does Sana's older sister react when she sees what Sana has done? *(She shouts her name in an angry way.)*

FOLLOW-UP: How would you react if this happened to you? Explain. *(I would act exactly the same way. Sana had already eaten her lollipop. She should not have eaten her sister's.)*

ASK: How is this the same as or different from what you predicted would happen on page 21? *(This is different because I thought Sana would ask to share her sister's lollipop, but she ate it without asking instead!)*

DOK 3

I hear a sound in the front hall closet. I should have known. That's where she always hides.

I shove aside the coats and boots. "I'm going to *get* you!"

Quick as a rat, she scoots through my legs and runs around and around the living room, the dining room, the kitchen, yelling, "Ami! Ami! Help! Help!"

23

READ FOR UNDERSTANDING

ASK: How does the illustration help you understand what happened next? *(It shows Sana's big sister chasing her; it shows where they ran in the house.)*

ANNOTATION TIP: Have children underline what Sana's big sister says. Have them circle what Sana says.

FOLLOW-UP: How will the way Sana's big sister speaks on this page be different from the way Sana speaks? *(Sana's big sister will speak in an angry way. Sana will sound like she is scared and needs help.)*

DOK 3

READ FOR UNDERSTANDING

ASK: What do you learn on this page that makes it easier to speak about who is telling the story? *(Sana calls her big sister by her name, Rubina. Rubina is telling the story.)*

DOK 2

READ FOR UNDERSTANDING

Monitor and Clarify

ASK: What question can you ask that helps you understand how Rubina is feeling? *(Possible response: Why doesn't Rubina cry after her mother tells her to share her lollipop?)*

FOLLOW-UP: Use what you know about Rubina to answer your question. *(Possible response: Rubina does what her mother asks her to do. Even though Rubina is upset that her mother is yelling at her, she doesn't cry.)*

DOK 3

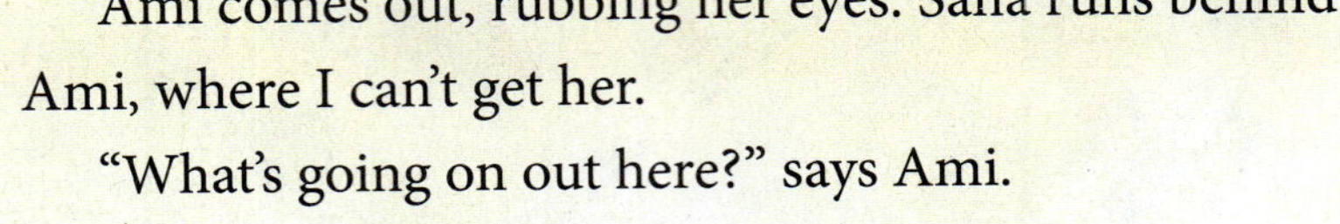

Ami comes out, rubbing her eyes. Sana runs behind Ami, where I can't get her.

"What's going on out here?" says Ami.

Sana says, "Rubina's trying to get me!"

Ami puts her hands on her hips. "Are you trying to get your little sister again?"

"She ate my *lollipop*! The greedy thing! She ate it!"

Ami says, "For shame! It's just a lollipop! Can't you *share* with your little sister?"

I want to cry, but I don't.

Sana runs to the fridge and brings back the triangle stuck to the stick. "Look! I didn't eat *all* of your lollipop! I left the triangle for you!"

"See?" says Ami. "She didn't eat *all* of it. She's sharing with you! Go ahead. Take the triangle."

So I have to take it.

"Go ahead. *Eat* the triangle."

But I don't. With all my might, I throw it across the room. It skitters under the sofa.

Sana scurries after it and eats that too.

READ FOR UNDERSTANDING

Quick Teach Words

As needed to support comprehension, briefly explain the meaning of *skitters* in context.

- When something *skitters* across the floor, it moves quickly and lightly.

READ FOR UNDERSTANDING

Monitor and Clarify

ASK: What question can you ask to make sure you understand Rubina's actions? *(Possible response: Why does Rubina feel that she has to take the lollipop but then throw it with all her might across the room?)*

FOLLOW-UP: Reread the text to answer your question. *(Possible response: Her mother tells her to take the lollipop because Sana is sharing it with her. She does what she is told to do but when asked to eat the triangle, she just can't. That's when she loses her temper and throws the lollipop.)*

DOK 3

READ FOR UNDERSTANDING

Monitor and Clarify

MODEL MONITORING AND CLARIFYING

THINK ALOUD *I ask myself: Why doesn't Rubina explain to her friends why she asked that her younger sister be invited to the party? Rubina looks so upset but doesn't do anything to help her friends understand why she did what she did. Then I remember that the only reason she made the telephone call was because her mother asked her to. Rubina does what her mother wants her to do and does not want to speak badly of her mother.*

DOK 3

The worst thing is that all the girls at school know if they invite me to their birthday parties, I have to bring Sana.

I don't get any invitations for a really long time.

26

Then one day Sana comes home waving an invitation.

"Ami! I've been invited to a birthday party! There's going to be games and toys and cake and ice cream! Can I go?"

Our little sister Maryam screams, "I wanna go too!" Sana says, "No! I can't take *her*! She's not invited!"

27

READ FOR UNDERSTANDING

ASK: How is this event the same as what happened at the beginning of the story? *(At the beginning of the story Rubina gets an invitation and Sana wants to go to the party, too. Now the same thing happens to Sana. She gets an invitation and her younger sister Maryam wants to go to the party, too.)*

FOLLOW-UP: What do you think will happen next? *(Possible response: Ami will tell Sana that she has to take Maryam to the party.)*

DOK 2

 READ FOR UNDERSTANDING

Monitor and Clarify

ASK: How does the illustration help you understand why Rubina says, "Leave me out of it." *(Possible response: The illustration shows Rubina thinking about what she should do. She pictures in her mind going to the party with her two younger sisters and then decides that she does not want to go.)*

DOK 3

Ami says, "Well . . . it's only fair. You went to Rubina's friend's party, now Rubina and Maryam can go to your friend's party."

I say, "Leave me out of it."

28

READ FOR UNDERSTANDING

ASK: What is your reaction to what Ami tells Sana? *(Possible response: Ami is treating Sana the same way she treated Rubina. She tells her that she has to take her younger sister to the party.)*

DOK 3

Now it's Sana's turn to beg and plead. Ami won't listen.

Sana's begging so hard she's crying, but still Ami won't listen.

I *could* just watch her have to take Maryam. I *could* just let her make a fool of herself at that party. I *could* just let her not be invited to any more parties, but something makes me tap Ami on the shoulder.

"What?"

"Don't make Sana take Maryam to the party."

30

Notice & Note

Contrasts and Contradictions

- **Remind children** that when characters act in a way that isn't expected, they should stop to notice and note.
- **Have children** explain why they might use this strategy on page 30. *(Instead of letting Sana look silly taking Maryam to the party—the way she had felt earlier in the story—Rubina takes Sana's side and asks Ami not to make Sana take Maryam to the party.)*

ANNOTATION TIP: Have children underline the parts of what Rubina said that they found surprising.

- **Remind them** of the Anchor Question: **Why would the character act this way?** *(Even though Sana behaved badly earlier in the story, Rubina still felt bad for her. She didn't want Sana to feel embarrassed like she had felt.)*

DOK 3

"No?" says Ami.
"No," I say.
Ami thinks for a moment, then says, "Okay."
So Sana gets to go by herself.

31

 READ FOR UNDERSTANDING

Phonics/Decoding in Context

Review that a final blend is a consonant pair at the end of a word. Both sounds in the blend can be heard. Have children point to the word *moment* and identify the consonants that make up the final blend. **Model blending** the sounds to demonstrate how each sound can be heard. Then have children blend and say the word with you.

 READ FOR UNDERSTANDING

ASK: Why does Ami change her mind? Use details from the text and the illustration. *(Possible response: The illustration shows Ami listening carefully to what Rubina said. She may remember that having Sana go to the party with Rubina caused problems. Ami realizes that there may be a different way to do things.)*

FOLLOW-UP: How is this the same as or different from your prediction on page 27? *(It is different. I thought she'd make Sana take Maryam.)*

DOK 3

READ FOR UNDERSTANDING

ASK: Why do you think Sana gave Rubina a green lollipop? *(Possible response: She feels bad for eating Rubina's lollipop before so she's giving Rubina her lollipop now.)*

FOLLOW-UP: Why does Rubina's and Sana's relationship change? *(Rubina and Sana are friends because they have had the same experiences. They have learned to help each other and be grateful for each other.)*

DOK 3

READ FOR UNDERSTANDING

Wrap Up

Revisit the predictions children made before reading. Have them confirm or correct their predictions using evidence from the text and pictures.

DOK 2

After the party, I hear a knock on my door.

"What do *you* want?" I ask Sana.

"Here." She hands me a big green lollipop. "This is for you."

"Thanks," I say.

After that we're friends.

32

Respond to Reading

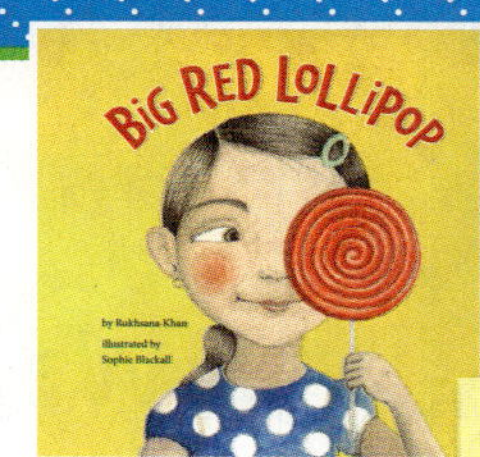

Use details from *Big Red Lollipop* to answer these questions with a partner.

1. **Monitor and Clarify** How did using what you know about birthday parties help you understand the events in the story?
2. How did the other girls at the party feel about Rubina bringing Sana? Use details from the text and pictures to explain your answer.
3. Why do you think Rubina tells Ami to let Sana go to the party without Maryam? What does that tell you about Rubina?

Listening Tip

Look at your partner as you listen. Wait until your partner finishes speaking before you talk.

Academic Discussion

Use the TURN AND TALK routine. Remind children to follow agreed-upon rules for discussions, such as sharing what they know about the topics under discussion and speaking clearly when they work with partners.

Possible responses:

1. *Accept reasonable responses.* DOK 3
2. *Rubina says that she knows Sally thinks it's weird that she has to bring Sana. Sally's face in the illustration on page 18 looks a little unsure. Rubina also says that the other girls know that she will always have to bring Sana along, so she doesn't get party invitations for a long time.* DOK 2
3. *Rubina knows what it feels like to take her little sister to a birthday party. She doesn't want Sana to feel the same way. This tells me that Rubina cares about Sana even though she has annoyed her in the past.* DOK 3

Respond to Reading

Write a Journal Entry

PROMPT How would the story be different if Sana were telling it? Think about the story events as you explain your ideas.

PLAN First, choose one event in the story to write about. Fill in the chart with what Sana does, says, and feels during that event.

Actions	Words	Feelings

34

Write About Reading

- **Read aloud** the prompt.
- **Lead a discussion** in which children discuss the differences between Rubina's and Sana's points of view. Tell them to use text evidence to support their ideas.
- Then read aloud the Plan section. Have children use their notes and ideas from the discussion to complete the chart.

DOK 3

WRITE Now write a journal entry from Sana's point of view that describes the event. Remember to:

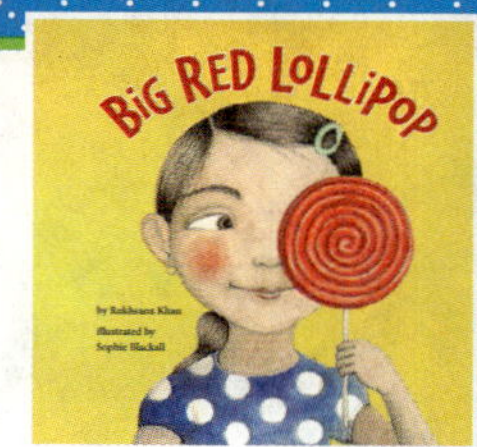

- Include details that show what Sana does, says, and feels.
- Use the words *I* and *me* to tell the story as Sana would.

Responses will vary.

35

Write About Reading

- **Read aloud** the Write section.
- **Encourage children** to make their writing sound like Sana is writing it in her journal.
- **Remind children** that their entry should describe the events in the story as seen through the eyes of Sana. Descriptive details should help readers understand more about Sana and how the story events made her feel.

DOK 3

Independent Close Reading

Have children close read and annotate "The Best Name" on their own during small-group or independent work time. As needed, **use the Scaffolded Support notes** that follow to guide children who need additional help.

Scaffolded Support

As needed, remind children to:

- pause as they read to make sure they understand what they are reading. They can reread, think about their own experiences, look at pictures, or ask themselves questions to monitor and clarify their understanding.
- find details in the text to decide who the narrator in the story is and from whose point of view the story is written.

DOK 2

Prepare to Read

GENRE STUDY **Realistic fiction** stories are made up but could happen in real life.

MAKE A PREDICTION Preview "The Best Name." In this story, a family has a new pet dog. They also have a problem. What do you think it is?

I think they need to decide what to name the dog.

SET A PURPOSE Read to find out how a family works together to solve a problem and to see if your prediction is correct. If not, use what you know about realistic fiction to make a new prediction.

36

The Best Name

READ As you read, ask yourself questions about parts that don't make sense. Then go back and reread those parts.

We just got a dog. He is so lovable! He has a very sweet face and a shiny red coat. The only problem is what to name him. Everyone in the family has an opinion. Dad wants Rolf because that is how the dog's bark sounds. Mom thinks he looks like an Ernie. My brother Sam wants to call him Digger. I want to let the dog pick, but I'm not sure how to do it.

Close Reading Tip

Underline the problem in the story.

CHECK MY UNDERSTANDING

How does the family feel about their dog? How can you tell?

They love him. The girl says he has a sweet face and he is lovable.

Scaffolded Support

As needed, remind children that:

- marking parts of the text they have questions about will allow them to return to those parts to see if their questions were answered.
- they can often identify how characters feel about something by looking closely at what the characters say and how they describe the object.

DOK 2

Close Reading Tip

Write **C** when you make a connection.

Scaffolded Support

As needed, remind children that:

- in a story, the narrator tells what happens. The narrator is also a character in the story when he or she uses first-person pronouns such as *I*, *me*, *my*, *we*, and *our* to talk about himself or herself.
- thinking about how an event in a story reminds them of something that happened in their own life or in another story they read can help them better understand the story and predict how the problem might be solved.

DOK 2

READ Who solves the problem? Underline the solution.

"Family meeting!" Mom announces when we sit at the table for dinner. "We're not going anywhere," she says, "until we all agree on a name for our dog."

Everyone argues for the name they like best.

"I know!" I say. "We can use all the names! We can use the *R* from Rolf, the *E* from Ernie, and the *D* from Digger!"

"RED!" everyone shouts together.

Red barks and wags his tail. We all laugh.

"Looks like we have a winner!" Dad says.

CHECK MY UNDERSTANDING

Who is the narrator? How does this point of view help you understand the story?

The big sister is telling the story. It helps me understand because she tells how she feels about the story events.

Cite Text Evidence

WRITE ABOUT IT How would the story be different if it were written from Red's point of view? Describe the events the way Red would. Include details about what he thinks, does, and feels.

My new family is so lovable. I wish they would think of a name for me. During dinner, I wait by the table for a snack. They talk about what to name me. I tell them I like the name Red. They agree.

39

Scaffolded Support

As needed, guide children to look for details that indicate how Red might feel about the story events and characters described in the original story, and then rewrite the story from his point of view.

DOK 3

Guided Practice

Prepare to Read

GENRE STUDY **Informational text** is nonfiction. It gives facts about a topic. As you read *Working with Others,* look for:

- the main topic and details
- headings that stand out
- photographs

SET A PURPOSE You know that informational texts include facts. Make a **prediction,** or good guess, about the information you will read about in this text. Read to see if your prediction is right. If not, make a new prediction.

POWER WORDS

- blamed
- argue
- respectful
- practice

Build Background: Teamwork and Cooperation

READ FOR UNDERSTANDING

Introduce the Text

- **Read aloud** and discuss the information about the genre.
- **Guide children** to set a purpose for reading to make and confirm predictions.
- **Provide information** about the background topic, Teamwork and Cooperation.
- **Tell children** to look for and think about the Power Words as they read.

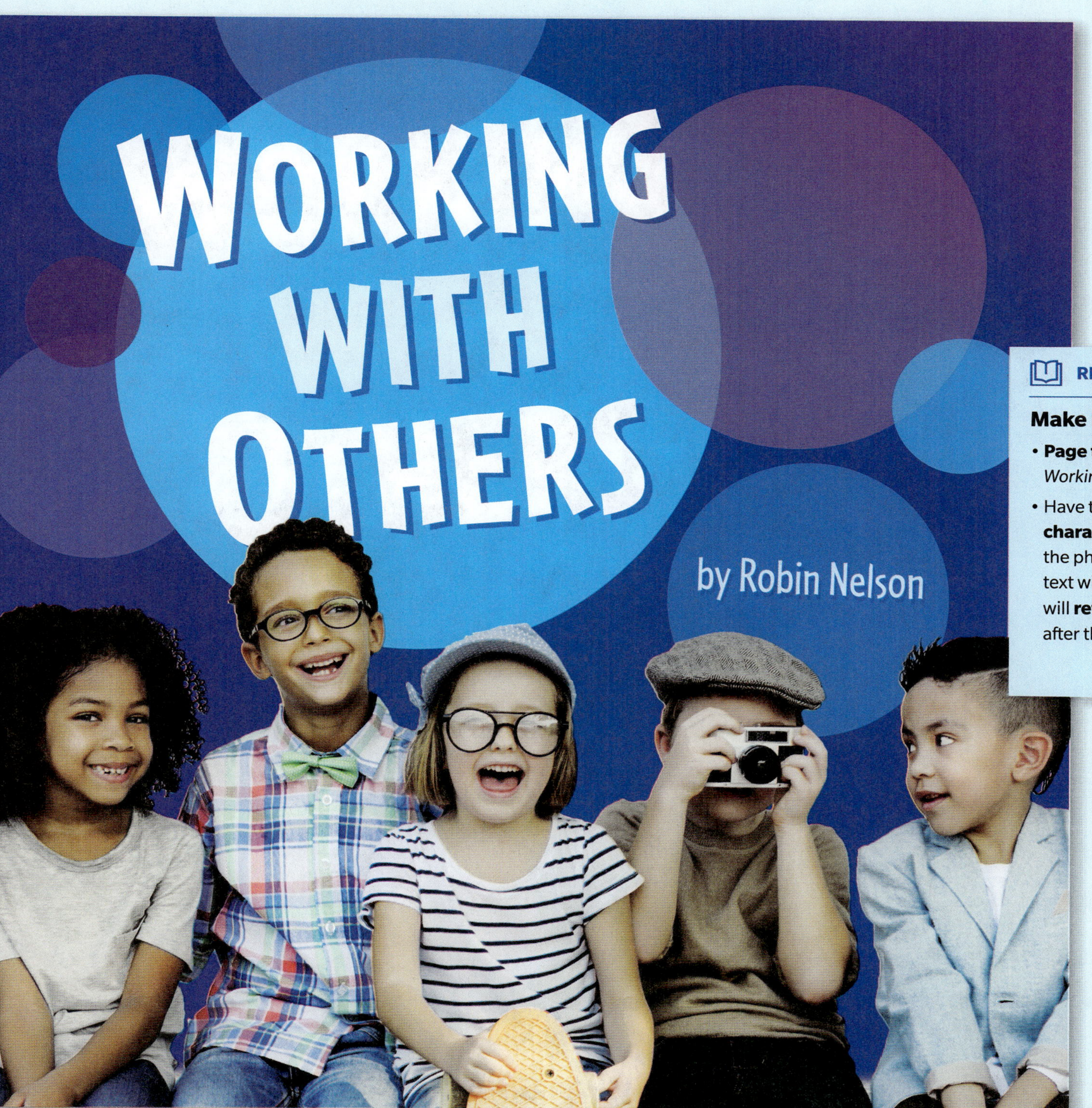

READ FOR UNDERSTANDING

Make Predictions

- **Page through** the beginning of *Working with Others* with children.
- Have them **use prior knowledge, characteristic of the genre,** and the photographs to predict what the text will be about. Tell children they will **return to their predictions** after they finish reading the text.

DOK 2

READ FOR UNDERSTANDING

ASK: What is the paragraph mostly about? Use your own words to summarize. *(Possible response: Most of the time you get along with the people you work and play with. Sometimes you do not.)*

DOK 2

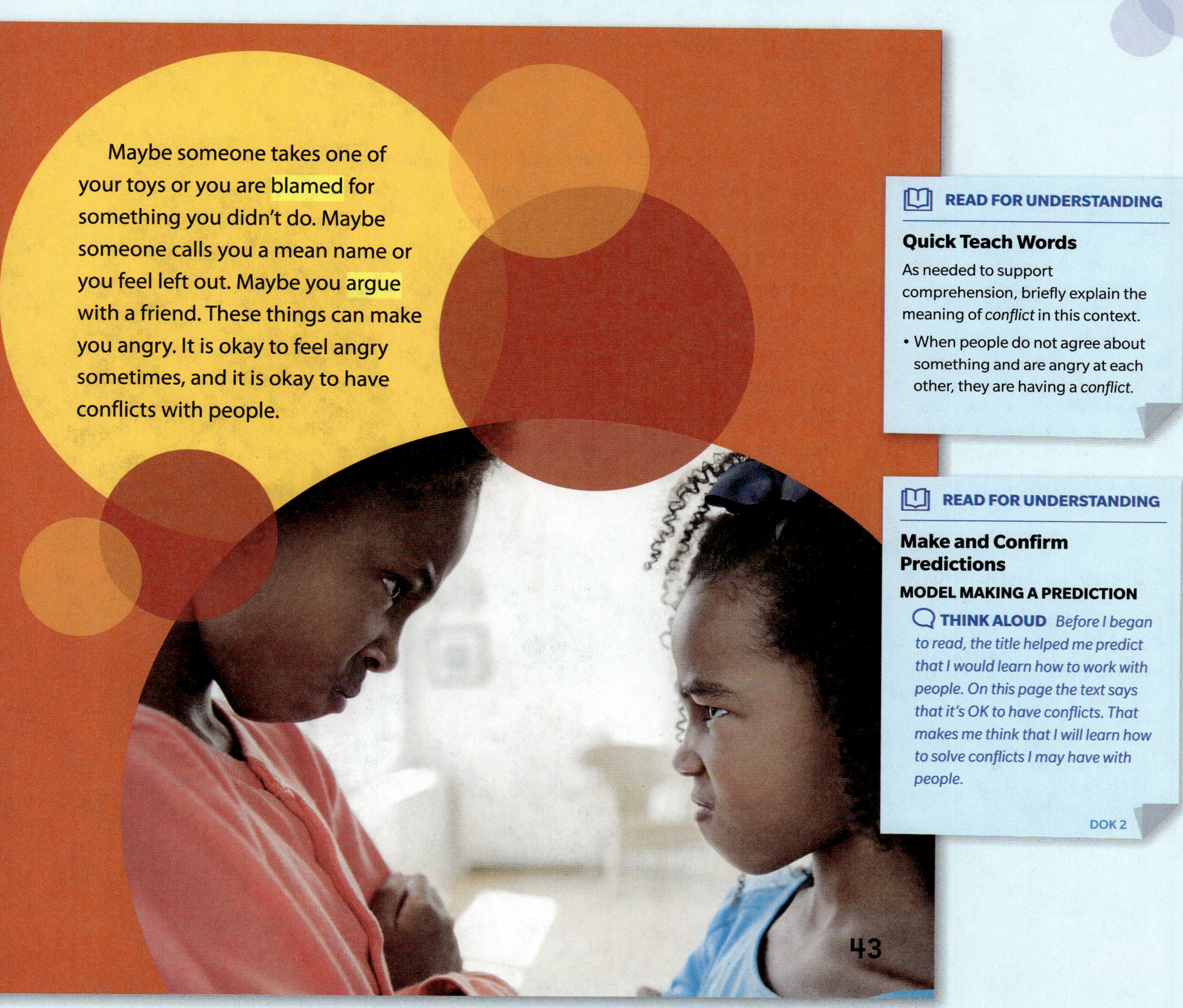
Maybe someone takes one of your toys or you are blamed for something you didn't do. Maybe someone calls you a mean name or you feel left out. Maybe you argue with a friend. These things can make you angry. It is okay to feel angry sometimes, and it is okay to have conflicts with people.

43

READ FOR UNDERSTANDING

Quick Teach Words

As needed to support comprehension, briefly explain the meaning of *conflict* in this context.

- When people do not agree about something and are angry at each other, they are having a *conflict*.

READ FOR UNDERSTANDING

Make and Confirm Predictions

MODEL MAKING A PREDICTION

THINK ALOUD *Before I began to read, the title helped me predict that I would learn how to work with people. On this page the text says that it's OK to have conflicts. That makes me think that I will learn how to solve conflicts I may have with people.*

DOK 2

READ FOR UNDERSTANDING

ASK: What is this paragraph mostly about? *(what some people do when conflicts make them angry)*

FOLLOW-UP: Which way has the girl in the photograph chosen to deal with her anger? Tell why you think so. *(I think the girl walked away from a conflict. She looks angry and upset. She is alone because she wants to calm down.)*

DOK 2

READ FOR UNDERSTANDING

Phonics/Decoding in Context

Have children point to the word *yell*. Review that when a one-syllable word ends with the sound for *l*, *s*, *t*, or *f*, the sound is sometimes spelled with two letters. **Model blending** the sounds in the word: /y/ /e/ /l/, *yell*. Have children repeat.

What do people do when conflicts make them angry? Some people yell and scream when they feel angry. Some people even hit other people. Yelling, screaming, and hitting do not solve conflicts. They hurt people and make problems worse. Some people walk away from conflicts. They want to be alone when they feel angry. They need time to calm down.

44

Walking away is okay at first. But it won't solve anything. People need to work things out with each other. People should talk about their feelings. Talking can solve conflicts. Talking can make everyone feel better.

We can solve conflicts without arguing. Take turns talking to let everyone share his or her opinion. Sometimes you will not agree with a person's opinion. Listen to what the other person is saying and ask questions.

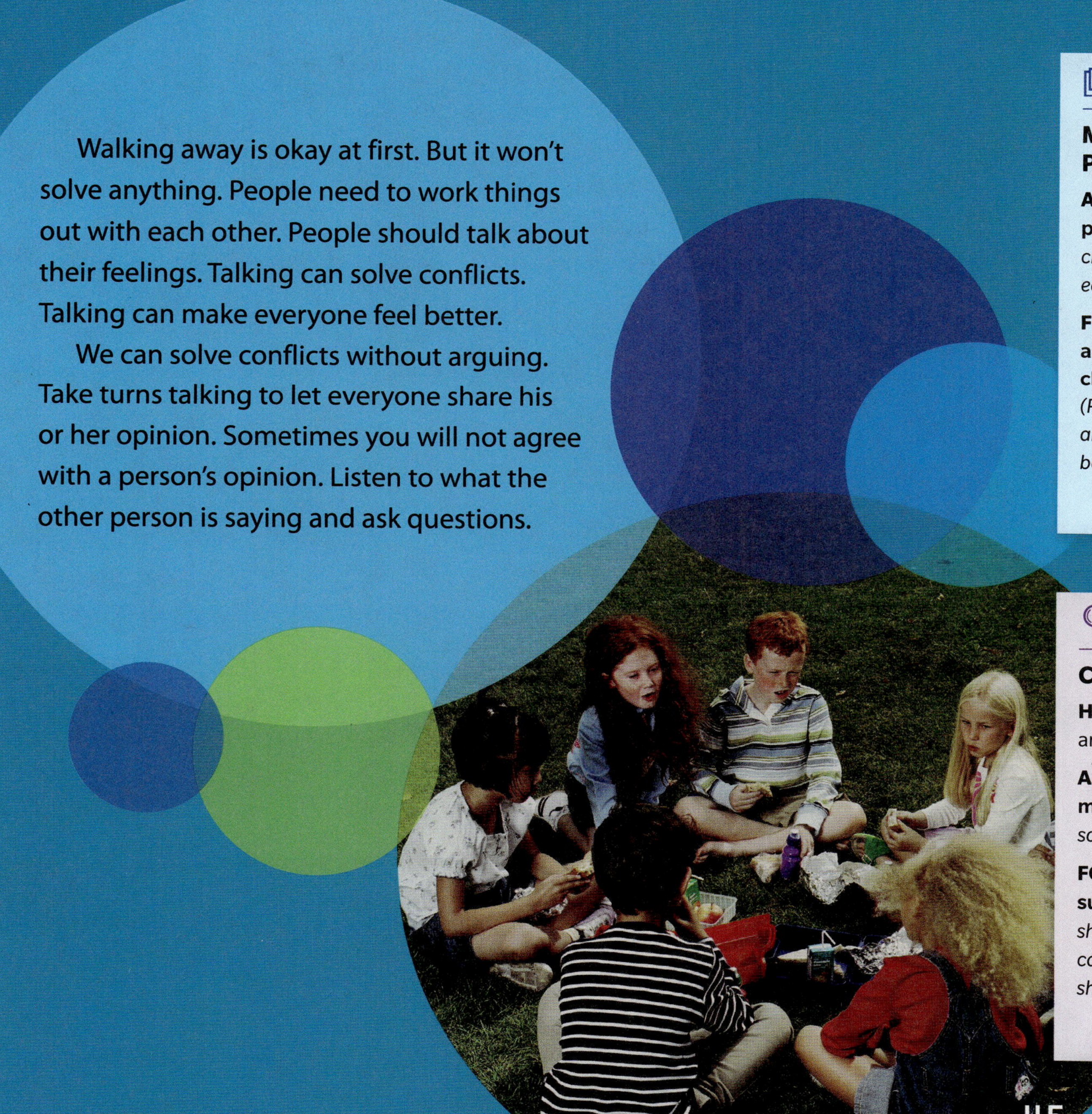

45

READ FOR UNDERSTANDING

Make and Confirm Predictions

ASK: What is the purpose of the photograph? *(to show how a group of children work things out by talking to each other)*

FOLLOW-UP: Have you learned anything that makes you want to change the prediction you made? *(Possible response: No. I am reading about how to solve conflicts to work better with people.)*

DOK 2

TARGETED CLOSE READ

Central Idea

Have children reread page 45 to analyze a central idea.

ASK: What are the two paragraphs mostly about? *(talking helps people solve problems)*

FOLLOW-UP: What evidence supports this central idea? *(People should talk about their feelings. Talking can help everyone feel better. You can share your opinion when you talk.)*

DOK 2

 READ FOR UNDERSTANDING

Phonics/Decoding in Context

Have children point to the word *call.* Say the word aloud and have them identify the end consonant sound and how it is spelled. **Model blending** the sounds in the word: /c/ /ô/ /l/, *call.* Have children repeat. As time allows, have children find a second word on the page that ends with a double consonant *(will),* identify the end sound and spelling, and read the word.

 READ FOR UNDERSTANDING

Make and Confirm Predictions

THINK ALOUD *The information on this page confirms my earlier prediction. The author does give details about ways to solve a conflict. Talking helps solve conflicts and gives everyone a chance to express their ideas and come up with a solution together.*

DOK 2

Use respectful words. Don't call each other names. Apologize when you are wrong. Make sure everyone has a chance to speak. Then you can solve conflicts together. Think of ideas to solve the conflicts. Decide which ideas will work best.

46

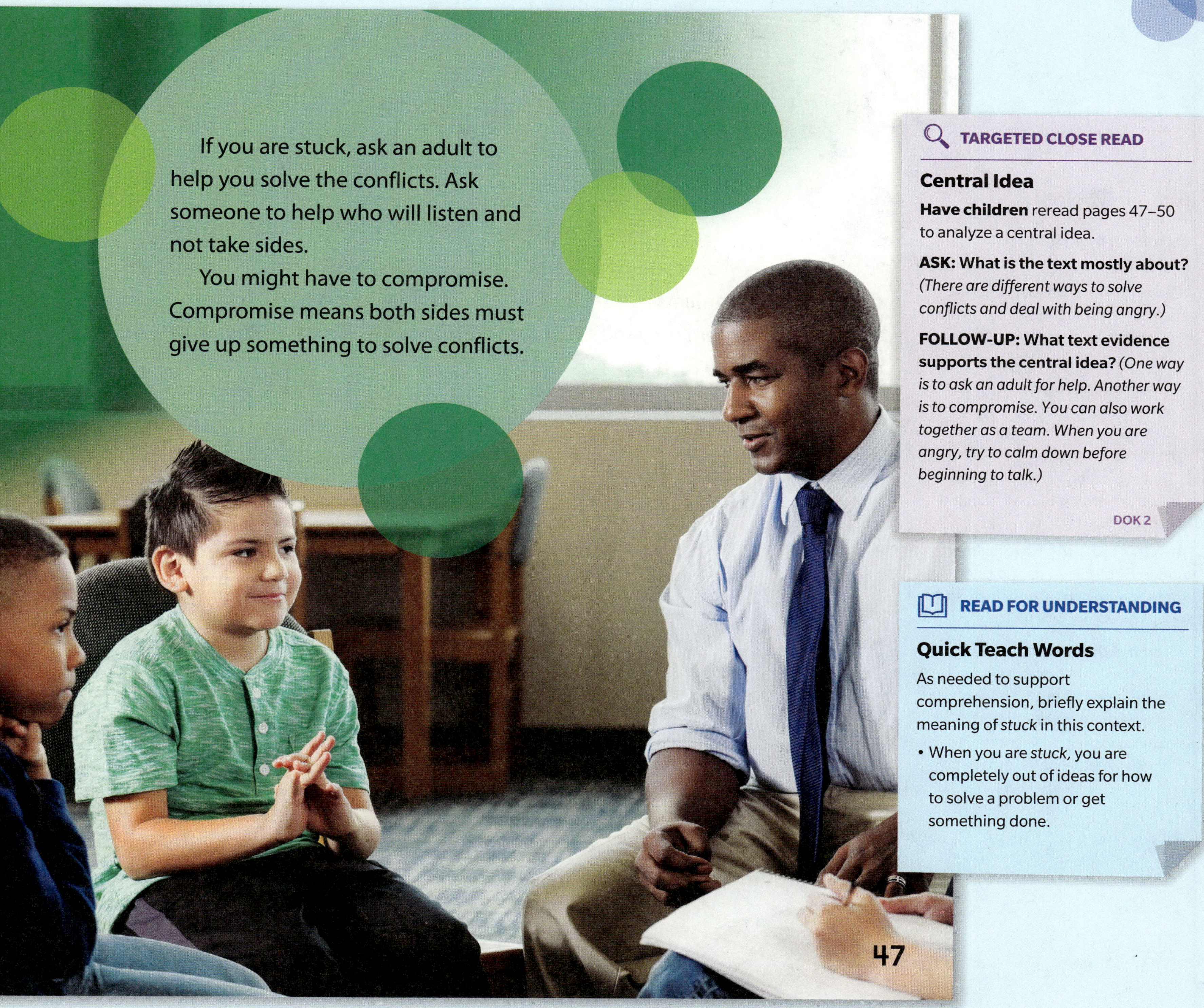

TARGETED CLOSE READ

Central Idea

Have children reread pages 47–50 to analyze a central idea.

ASK: What is the text mostly about? *(There are different ways to solve conflicts and deal with being angry.)*

FOLLOW-UP: What text evidence supports the central idea? *(One way is to ask an adult for help. Another way is to compromise. You can also work together as a team. When you are angry, try to calm down before beginning to talk.)*

DOK 2

READ FOR UNDERSTANDING

Quick Teach Words

As needed to support comprehension, briefly explain the meaning of *stuck* in this context.

- When you are *stuck*, you are completely out of ideas for how to solve a problem or get something done.

Extreme or Absolute Language

- **Remind children** that when an author uses language that clearly tells what he or she thinks, they should stop to notice and note.
- **Have children** explain why they might use this strategy on page 48. *(The author says that if you can talk a conflict out, "everyone" will be happy. That tells me how important the author thinks it is to solve a conflict peacefully.)*

ANNOTATION TIP: Have children underline other words and phrases that show how the author feels about solving conflicts peacefully.

- **Remind them** of the Anchor Question: **What does this make me wonder about?** *(I wonder what happens when talking about a conflict does not solve the problem. What should people do then?)*

DOK 3

Solving conflicts peacefully takes practice. Work together! Solve conflicts as a team. Talk them out, and everyone will be happy!

48

Dealing with Anger

What do you do when you feel angry? You might feel too angry to talk about how you feel. Here are some ways for you to calm down and get the anger out.

- Take deep breaths and count slowly.
- Write down what happened and how you feel about it.
- Draw a picture.
- Listen to calm music.
- Read a book.
- Take a walk or do some other kind of exercise.
- Pound on a pillow.
- Stomp your feet.

READ FOR UNDERSTANDING

ASK: Why do you think the author put this information in a list? *(The tips are ways that people can calm down and feel better when they are angry. Showing them in a list makes it easier to read each one and think about how it might be helpful.)*

FOLLOW-UP: Why are these tips helpful to people who are trying to solve a conflict? *(They help people feel less angry. When you are not angry, you can solve a conflict in a more peaceful way.)*

DOK 3

READ FOR UNDERSTANDING

Make and Confirm Predictions

ANNOTATION TIP: Have children circle the heading on this page.

ASK: How does the heading help you predict what you will learn on this page? *(Possible response: I know that talking things out is one way to solve a conflict. I think I will read advice about what people who are having a conflict can say as they talk things out.)*

DOK 2

READ FOR UNDERSTANDING

Wrap Up

Revisit the predictions children made before reading. Have them confirm or correct their predictions using evidence from the text and illustrations.

DOK 2

Talking Things Out

When you feel a little better, it is time to talk. Here are some things to remember when talking things out.

- Tell the other person how you feel and why you feel that way. Be honest. Ask that person how he or she feels.
- Remember that your body also tells a person how you are feeling. Show that you care about what he or she is saying. Don't cross your arms or make faces.
- Look at the person you are speaking to. Do the same thing when the other person is speaking to you.
- Listen carefully to what the other person has to say.
- Wait for your turn to speak.
- Apologize when you are wrong or if you hurt someone's feelings.
- Try to find a way to do things differently next time.

50

Respond to Reading

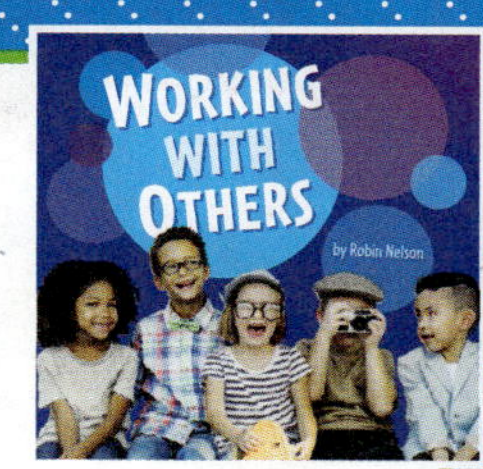

Use details from *Working with Others* to answer these questions with a partner.

1. **Make and Confirm Predictions** What predictions did you make about the facts you would read in this text? What were you right about? What was different?

2. Use information from the text to describe things that can cause a conflict.

3. Why is it a good idea to make sure that everyone has a chance to speak when solving conflicts?

Talking Tip

Ask to learn more about one of your partner's ideas. Complete the sentence below.

Please explain ________.

Academic Discussion

Use the TURN AND TALK routine. Remind children to follow agreed-upon rules for discussions, such as listening carefully to their partner and asking for clarification if they are unsure of an idea.

Possible responses:

1. *I predicted that the text would be about how it is better to work together. I changed my prediction because the text is also about what to do when it is hard to work together.* DOK 2
2. *Someone takes one of your toys, you are blamed for something you didn't do, you are called a mean name, you feel left out.* DOK 2
3. *Making sure that everyone speaks is a way for everyone to share an opinion. Then, together, you can work out a solution that is fair to everyone.* DOK 2

Respond to Reading

Write an Explanation

PROMPT How do you solve a conflict with someone? Use details from the words and photos to explain your answer.

PLAN First, make notes about steps you can follow when you are having a conflict.

Write About Reading

- **Read aloud** the prompt.
- **Lead a discussion** in which children share their ideas about solving a conflict. Tell them to use examples of ways to solve a conflict in the text and photos to support their ideas.
- Then read aloud the Plan section. Have children use ideas from the discussion to help them note steps in solving a conflict.

DOK 3

WRITE Now write an explanation that tells someone what to do to solve a conflict. Remember to:

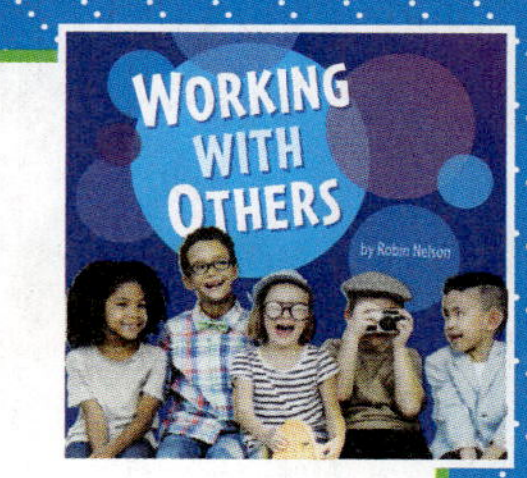

- Look for details in the text that are good examples of how to solve a conflict.
- Use action words that tell your reader exactly what to do.

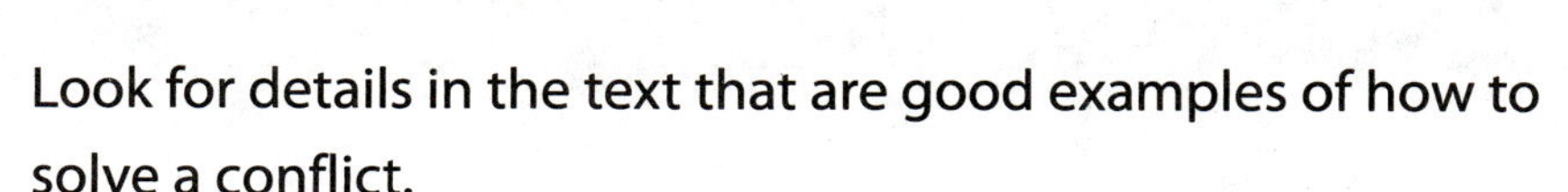

Write About Reading

- **Read aloud** the Write section.
- **Remind children** to think about good examples of solving a conflict from the text.
- **Encourage children** to use action words when describing ways to solve a conflict.

DOK 3

Independent Close Reading

Have children close read and annotate "I Respectfully Disagree!" on their own during small-group or independent work time. As needed, **use the Scaffolded Support notes** that follow to guide children who need additional help.

Scaffolded Support

As needed, remind children to:

- use text features, photos, and what they know about the genre to make a prediction before they begin reading. As they read, they can confirm their prediction or make a new one.
- look for important text details that help them figure out the central idea.

DOK 2

On My Own

Prepare to Read

GENRE STUDY **Informational text** is nonfiction. It gives facts about a topic.

MAKE A PREDICTION Preview "I Respectfully Disagree!" You know that informational text has facts and details about a topic. What do you think you'll learn from reading this text?

I think I will learn what to do when friends have different opinions.

SET A PURPOSE Read to find out how to respectfully disagree with someone.

54

I Respectfully Disagree!

READ What is the topic of this text?

Have you and a friend ever had different opinions about something? Of course you have! Everyone has an opinion. Sometimes a friend's opinion won't match yours. It is important to be respectful when this happens. Remember to be polite and caring. Just because he or she has a different opinion doesn't mean you can't still be friends!

Close Reading Tip

Circle words you don't know. Then figure them out. If you need to, look them up in a dictionary.

Scaffolded Support

As needed, remind children that:

- the topic of a text is what the text is mostly about. Thinking about which information and details are most important will help them identify and understand the topic.
- a dictionary can help them understand the meaning of a word when it is difficult to identify clues in the surrounding words or sentences.

DOK 2

CHECK MY UNDERSTANDING

What is the text mainly about?

Friends can have different opinions about things.

55

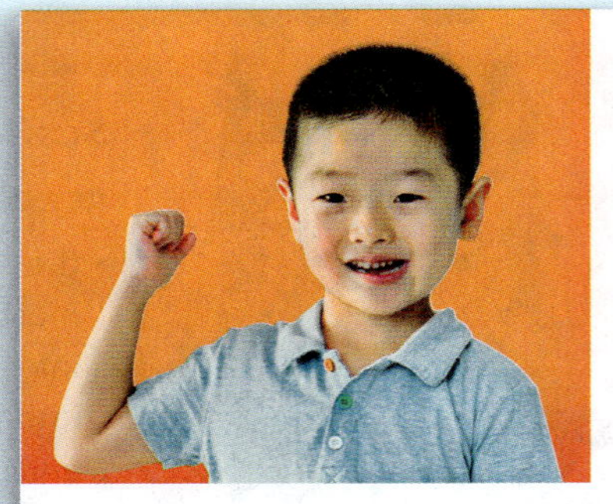

READ Underline the sentence that tells the central idea on this page. Which details tell more about the central idea?

It can be hard to understand why a friend doesn't share your opinion. However, don't call your friend names or say your friend is wrong. Just because a person has a different opinion doesn't mean it's wrong. Say "I respectfully disagree" and explain why. Sometimes, no matter what you say, you and your friend will not agree. It might be that the one thing you do agree on is that you disagree! In this case you can say, "Let's agree to disagree!"

Close Reading Tip

Mark important words with *.

Scaffolded Support

As needed, remind children that:

- the central idea is the most important idea about the topic. Thinking about important details in the text can help you arrive at the central idea.
- they will confirm or revise the predictions they made before reading using details from the text.

DOK 2

CHECK MY UNDERSTANDING

Look back at the prediction you made on page 54. Was it correct? Why or why not?

Responses will vary.

Cite Text Evidence

WRITE ABOUT IT Do you think knowing how to disagree respectfully is important? Why or why not? Use details from the text to explain your opinion.

I think it is important to disagree respectfully. It helps you stay friends. Saying "I respectfully disagree" and telling why is nicer than saying someone is wrong and calling him or her names. Sometimes it's okay to agree to disagree.

57

Scaffolded Support

As needed, guide children to use details from the text to support their opinions about the importance of disagreeing respectfully.

DOK 3

Guided Practice

Prepare to Read

GENRE STUDY **Biographies** tell about real people's lives. As you read *Gingerbread for Liberty!,* look for:

- information about why this person is important
- the place where the person lived, worked, or traveled
- ways the person has made a difference

SET A PURPOSE Read to find out the most important ideas in each part. Then **synthesize,** or put together these ideas in your mind, to find out what the text really means to you.

POWER WORDS

- booming
- skill
- threatening
- persuade

Meet Mara Rockliff.

READ FOR UNDERSTANDING

Introduce the Text

- **Read aloud** and discuss the information about the genre.
- **Guide children** to set a purpose for reading to practice synthesizing ideas in the text.
- **Provide information** about the author, Mara Rockliff.
- **Tell children** to look for and think about the Power Words as they read.

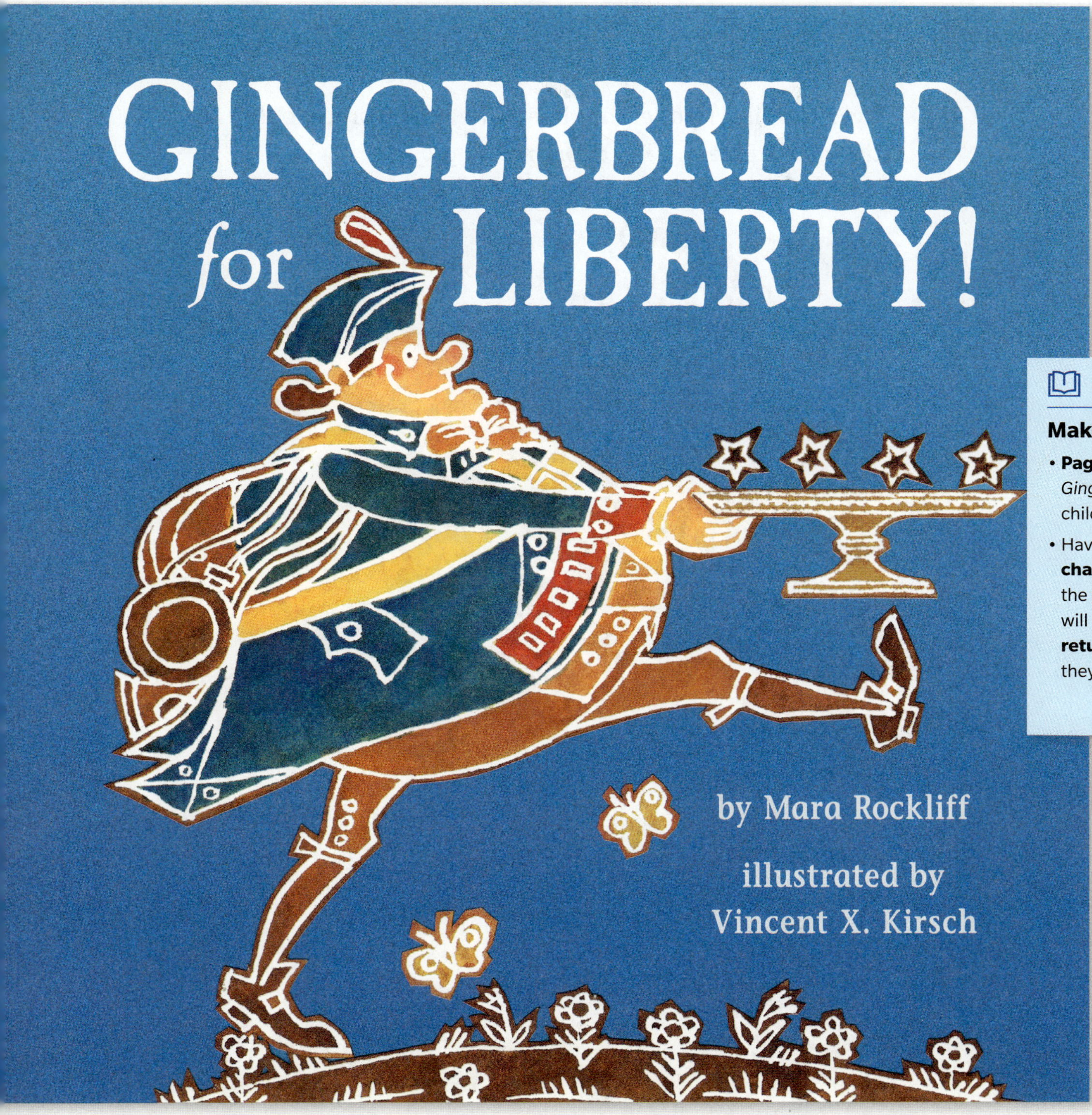

GINGERBREAD for LIBERTY!

by Mara Rockliff

illustrated by Vincent X. Kirsch

 **READ FOR UNDERSTANDING**

Make Predictions

- **Page through** the beginning of *Gingerbread for Liberty* with children.
- Have them **use prior knowledge, characteristics of the genre,** and the pictures to predict what the text will be about. Tell children they will **return to their predictions** after they finish reading.

DOK 2

Everyone in Philadelphia knew the gingerbread baker. His honest face . . . his booming laugh . . .

60

Notice & Note

Extreme or Absolute Language

- **Remind children** that when an author uses language that clearly says what he or she thinks, they should stop to notice and note.
- **Have children** explain why they might use this strategy on page 60. *(The author says that "everyone" in Philadelphia knew the gingerbread baker. This makes me think the author believes the baker was very popular and well-liked.)*

ANNOTATION TIP: Have children underline the extreme or absolute language used in the story.

- **Remind them** of the Anchor Question: **What does this make me wonder about?** *(Why was the baker so well known? How did he get so famous and popular?)*

DOK 3

And, of course, his gingerbread—the best in all the thirteen colonies. His big, floury hands turned out castles and queens, horses and cows and hens—each detail drawn in sweet, buttery icing with the greatest skill and care.

And yet, despite his care, there always seemed to be some broken pieces for the hungry children who followed their noses to the spicy-smelling shop.

"No empty bellies here!" the baker bellowed. "Not in *my* America!"

61

READ FOR UNDERSTANDING

ASK: How do the describing words help you understand the baker's skills? *(The describing words help me use my senses to imagine everything the baker made.)*

ANNOTATION TIP: Have children circle all the describing words on the page.

DOK 2

READ FOR UNDERSTANDING

ASK: What does the baker mean when he says, "No empty bellies here! Not in *my* America!" *(He won't let anyone go hungry if he can do something about it.)*

FOLLOW UP: What do these words tell you about the baker? *(He is kind and caring. He wants people to have a good life in America.)*

DOK 2

TARGETED CLOSE READ

Text Organization

Have children reread pages 62–64 to analyze how the text is organized.

ASK:

- **What happens on pages 62–64?** *(The baker moves to the New World to open his own bakery. He leaves home to join General Washington.)*
- **How are these events connected?** *(The baker wouldn't have gone to help General Washington if he hadn't moved to the New World.)*

FOLLOW-UP:

- **How are the events organized, and why do you think the author organized the events this way?** *(They are in the order they happened. The author organized the events this way so the reader knows the order the events happened and to make the events easier to follow and understand.)*

DOK 3

For once upon a time, he had been young and hungry too.

And he had followed his own nose to this New World, where a hard-working young man could open his own bakery and always have enough to eat.

62

But now, something was in the air (besides the smell of baking gingerbread).
Newspapers shouted

REVOLUTION! INDEPENDENCE! LIBERTY!

Boys rolled up blankets, shouldered guns, and kissed mothers goodbye.

The baker hung his apron up. He dusted flour off his hands.

"Where are you going?" asked his wife.

"To fight for my America!" he said. "I was a soldier once."

"That was long ago and far away," she said. "You are a baker now, and you are old and fat."

63

READ FOR UNDERSTANDING

Synthesize

ANNOTATION TIP: Have children circle the newspaper headlines.

ASK: What do you notice about the text on this page? *(Three of the words are larger. They are spelled with capital letters. An exclamation point follows each word.)*

FOLLOW-UP: How should you read these words? *(I should read them louder and with excitement. Each word should be a little louder since each word is bigger than the next.)*

MODEL SYNTHESIZING

THINK ALOUD *I am not certain I understand what is happening, so I will stop and ask myself the question: Why are the newspaper headlines important? The text helps me answer. Boys are going to fight for America. The headlines announce the beginning of America's war. They help me know this is big, important news. I see how the author helped me connect how this is something important because the newspaper headlines were yelling the news.*

DOK 3

The baker knew his wife was right.
But he knew also that he loved his country.
Somehow, he had to find a way to help.

He packed his bags and went to join General Washington.

64

READ FOR UNDERSTANDING

ASK: Where is the baker going? *(to join General Washington and fight in the war)*

FOLLOW-UP: Predict how the baker can help. *(Accept reasonable responses.)*

DOK 2

General Washington did not say the baker was old and fat. General Washington was too polite. Anyway, he had other troubles on his mind.

65

READ FOR UNDERSTANDING

ANNOTATION TIP: Have children circle what the soldiers say.

ASK: How does the illustration help you understand the "other troubles" George Washington has on his mind? *(The illustration shows what the American soldiers are saying to General Washington. They are hungry and don't have enough food. They are threatening to leave the army.)*

DOK 2

READ FOR UNDERSTANDING

Synthesize

ASK: What is the baker going to do? *(He is going to bake gingerbread for the soldiers.)*

FOLLOW-UP: How will this solve Washington's problem? *(The soldiers will not be hungry and will not want to leave the army.)* **How will it make the baker feel?** *(The baker will feel good because his baking will help General Washington and will keep people from being hungry.)*

DOK 2

The baker rolled up his sleeves.
"No empty bellies here," he told General Washington.
"Not in *my* America!"
But bigger trouble was on the way.

Across the ocean. . .

66

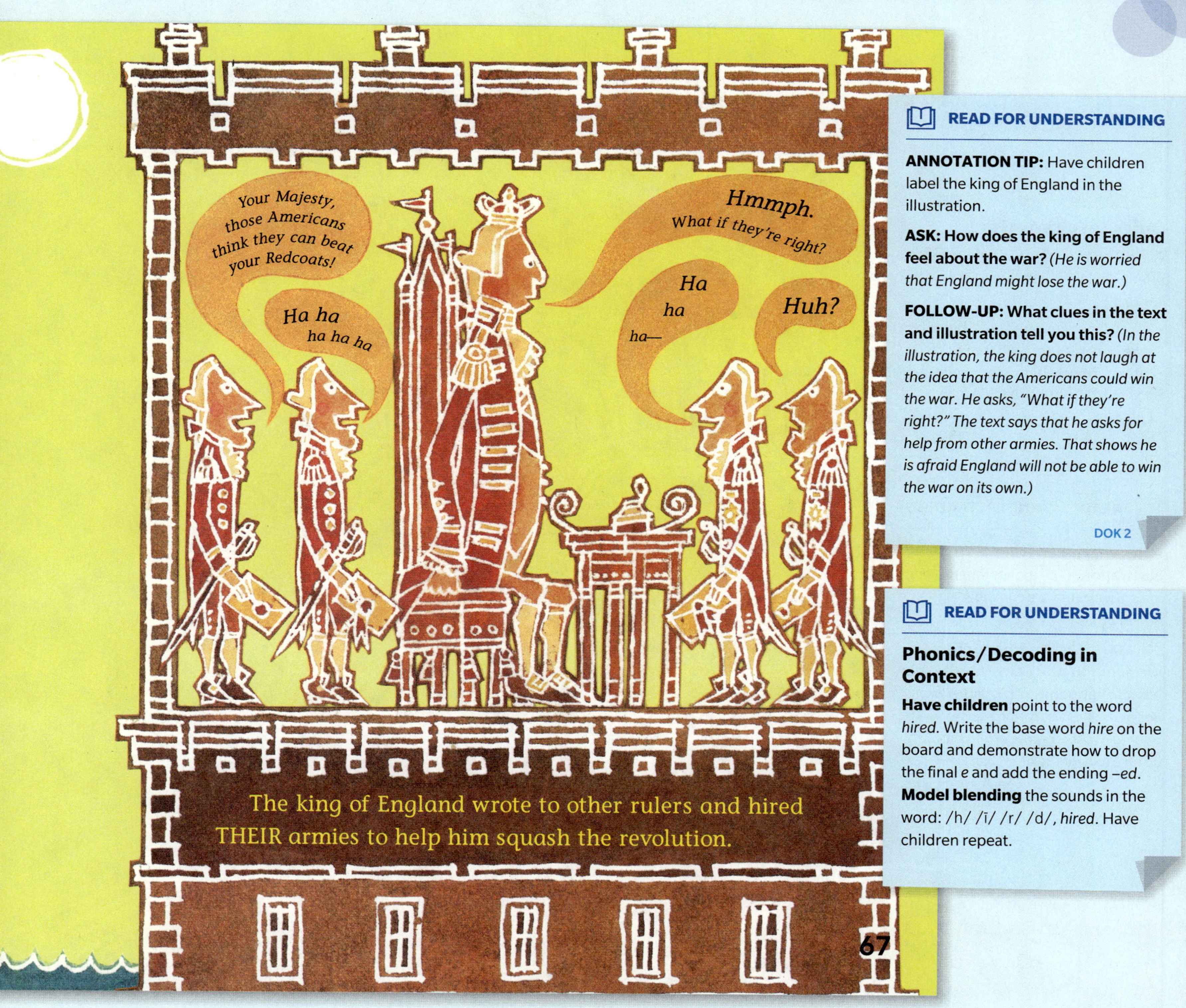

READ FOR UNDERSTANDING

ANNOTATION TIP: Have children label the king of England in the illustration.

ASK: How does the king of England feel about the war? *(He is worried that England might lose the war.)*

FOLLOW-UP: What clues in the text and illustration tell you this? *(In the illustration, the king does not laugh at the idea that the Americans could win the war. He asks, "What if they're right?" The text says that he asks for help from other armies. That shows he is afraid England will not be able to win the war on its own.)*

DOK 2

READ FOR UNDERSTANDING

Phonics/Decoding in Context

Have children point to the word *hired.* Write the base word *hire* on the board and demonstrate how to drop the final *e* and add the ending *-ed.* **Model blending** the sounds in the word: /h/ /ī/ /r/ /d/, *hired.* Have children repeat.

When the ships sailed into sight, even General Washington turned pale. Who had ever seen such an army?

 **READ FOR UNDERSTANDING**

Quick Teach Words

As needed to support comprehension, briefly explain the meaning of *pale* in context.

- When a person turns *pale*, his or her face becomes very white. People often turn pale when they have had a shock or fright of some kind.

 **READ FOR UNDERSTANDING**

ASK: What is happening in the illustration? *(The armies that the king of England hired are coming to fight the Americans.)*

FOLLOW-UP: Why does General Washington turn pale when he sees what is happening? *(The other army has many ships and many soldiers. General Washington is afraid they will be able to beat the Americans.)*

DOK 2

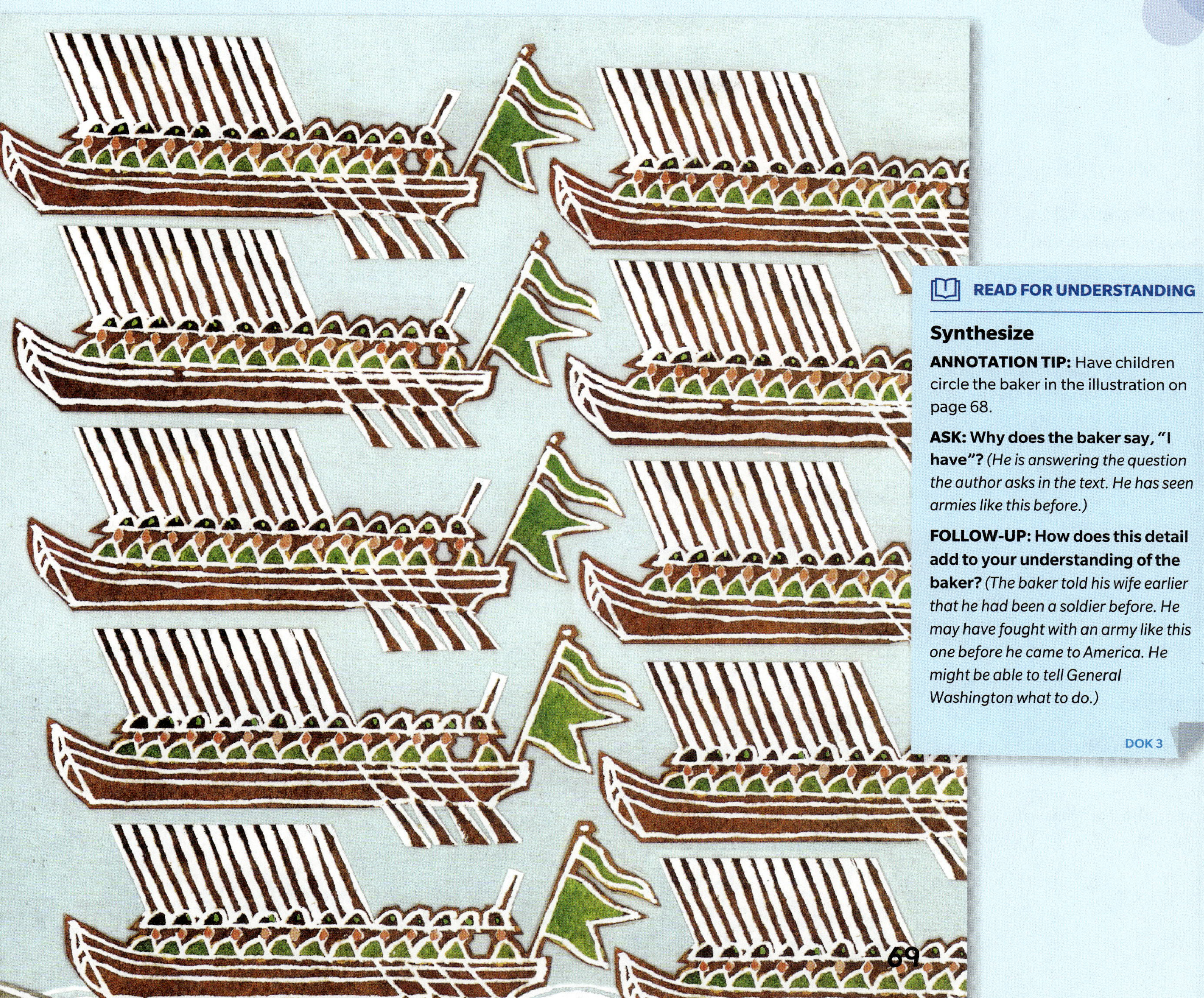

READ FOR UNDERSTANDING

Synthesize

ANNOTATION TIP: Have children circle the baker in the illustration on page 68.

ASK: Why does the baker say, "I have"? *(He is answering the question the author asks in the text. He has seen armies like this before.)*

FOLLOW-UP: How does this detail add to your understanding of the baker? *(The baker told his wife earlier that he had been a soldier before. He may have fought with an army like this one before he came to America. He might be able to tell General Washington what to do.)*

DOK 3

TARGETED CLOSE READ

Text Organization

Have children reread pages 70–75 to analyze text organization.

ANNOTATION TIP: Have children number each important event they described.

ASK: In your own words, tell what happens in this part of the story. *(First, the baker tells George Washington he wants to speak to the soldiers and persuade them that they are not enemies. Then the baker rows across the bay. He tells the hungry soldiers he has a bakeshop and that no one in his America is hungry. The soldiers must have switched sides because the Majesty is told the army has disappeared. After many battles the British surrender and the war is over.)*

FOLLOW-UP: How does the way this text is organized support the author's purpose for writing it? *(Telling the events in the order they happened supports the author's purpose of giving information about something that happened in history.)*

DOK 3

"These soldiers come from the land where I was born," the baker told General Washington. "Let me go speak to them. Perhaps I can persuade them we are not their enemies. Perhaps I can even persuade them to switch sides!"

"If you are caught, you will be killed," Washington warned.

The baker smiled. "Then I must not be caught."

70

In the darkest hour of the night, he rowed across the bay. With each dip of his oars, he thought of words to win the soldiers over to the American cause.

REVOLUTION! (splash)

Befreiung!

INDEPENDENCE! (splash)

Unabhängigkeit!

LIBERTY! (splash, splash)

Freiheit!

71

READ FOR UNDERSTANDING

ASK: Why is the baker rowing across the bay? *(He is going to try to convince the soldiers not to fight the Americans.)*

FOLLOW-UP: Why do you think this is important? *(The army coming to fight the Americans is too large. If soldiers don't switch to the American side, then the Americans will lose.)*

DOK 2

READ FOR UNDERSTANDING

ASK: Do you have any questions about the text on this page? *(Possible response: I wonder why some of the words are larger than others; I wonder what some of the words mean; I wonder if the word in larger type means the same thing as the word above it.)*

FOLLOW-UP: Why is the baker speaking in a different language? *(He says the soldiers are from the land where he was born. He knows they may not speak English if they are from countries hired by the king of England.)*

DOK 3

 READ FOR UNDERSTANDING

Phonics/Decoding in Context

Have children point to the word *rising*. Write the base word *rise* on the board and demonstrate how to drop the final *e* and add the ending *–ing*. **Model blending** the sounds in the word: /r/ /ī/ /z/ /i/ /ng/, *rising*. Have children repeat.

 READ FOR UNDERSTANDING

Quick Teach Words

As needed to support comprehension, briefly explain the meaning of *fragrant* in context.

- Something that is *fragrant* has a very light and pleasant smell.

But when he looked into their hungry faces, all his fine words slipped away.

What could he say?

"I have a bakeshop . . ." he began.

As the baker spoke, the soldiers seemed to see the fragrant steam rising from his ovens. They could almost smell the spicy gingerbread, and taste the sweet, buttery icing on their tongues.

72

"And you always have enough to eat?" the soldiers asked.

"No empty bellies here," the baker told them. "Not in *my* America!"

Across the ocean. . .

73

READ FOR UNDERSTANDING

Synthesize

ASK: Why did the baker tell the soldiers about his bakeshop? *(The baker saw how hungry the soldiers looked. He thought that if they knew they would have enough to eat, they might stop fighting the Americans.)*

FOLLOW-UP: How does this add to your understanding of the baker? *(It tells me that the baker is clever. He knows that the soldiers' need for food is greater than their need to fight.)*

DOK 2

READ FOR UNDERSTANDING

Synthesize

ASK: How can the words "Across the ocean" help you predict what will happen next? *(I know that England is across the Atlantic Ocean from America. That makes me think that the action will go back to England and the king.)*

DOK 2

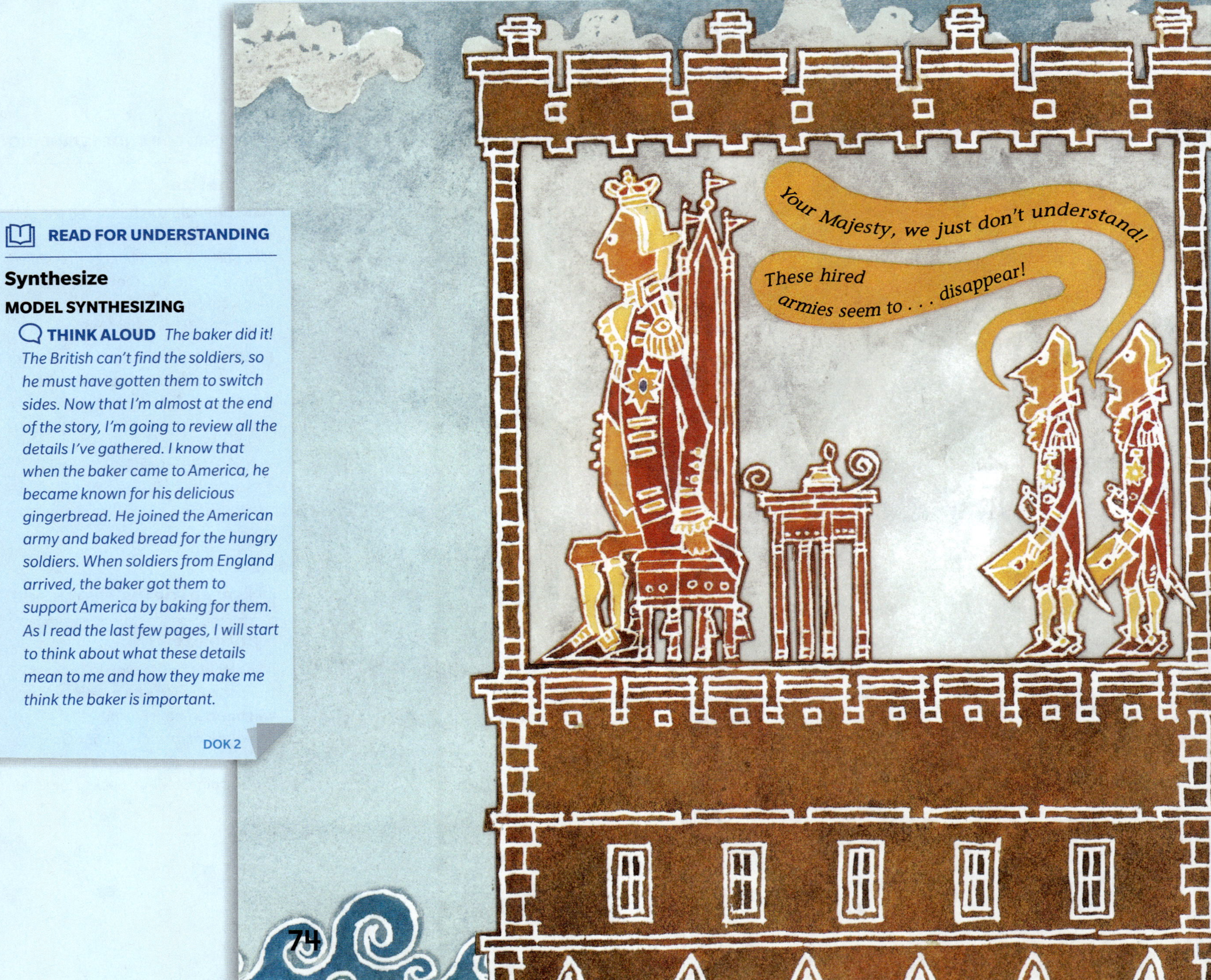

READ FOR UNDERSTANDING

Synthesize

MODEL SYNTHESIZING

THINK ALOUD *The baker did it! The British can't find the soldiers, so he must have gotten them to switch sides. Now that I'm almost at the end of the story, I'm going to review all the details I've gathered. I know that when the baker came to America, he became known for his delicious gingerbread. He joined the American army and baked bread for the hungry soldiers. When soldiers from England arrived, the baker got them to support America by baking for them. As I read the last few pages, I will start to think about what these details mean to me and how they make me think the baker is important.*

DOK 2

Many, many loaves—and battles!—later . . .

THE BRITISH HAVE SURRENDERED!
THE REVOLUTION IS OVER!
WE WON!

"My work is done!" the baker cried.

Washington said, "Not quite."

75

READ FOR UNDERSTANDING

ASK: How do you know that the war didn't end as soon as the soldiers switched sides? *(The text says, "Many, many loaves—and battles!—later." This tells me that the baker baked a lot of bread and the soldiers fought in many battles before the war ended.)*

DOK 2

Did he bake the British soldiers gingerbread for their dessert?

We'll never know . . .

They didn't leave a crumb.

76

READ FOR UNDERSTANDING

Synthesize

ASK: Synthesize the details you have learned about the baker. How do they help you understand why he was an important part of history? *(The baker played an important part in the Revolutionary War. His baking convinced the soldiers from his home country to support the Americans. If they hadn't switched sides, the Americans might not have won the war.)*

DOK 3

READ FOR UNDERSTANDING

Wrap Up

Revisit the predictions children made before reading. Have them confirm or correct their predictions using evidence from the text and pictures.

DOK 2

Respond to Reading

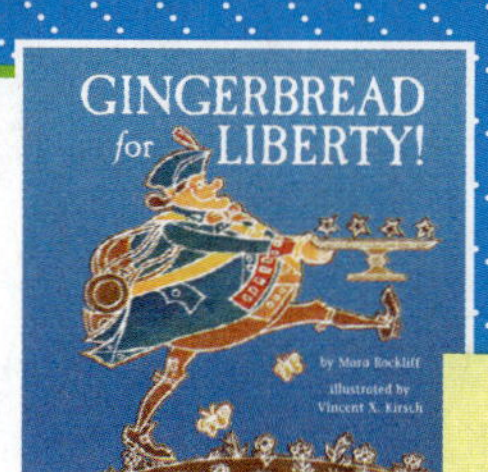

Use details from *Gingerbread for Liberty!* to answer these questions with a partner.

1. **Synthesize** Why did the baker want to join General Washington? How did that decision change history?

2. What does the author want to describe? What does the illustrator want to show?

3. How did General Washington's feelings about the baker change? What do you think Washington learned from this experience?

Listening Tip

Look at your partner as you listen. Nod your head to show you are interested.

Academic Discussion

Use the TURN AND TALK routine. Remind children to follow agreed-upon discussion rules, such as nodding their head to show they are interested in what their partner is saying.

Possible responses:

1. *He loved his country and wanted to fight for America. If he hadn't joined the army, the German soldiers might have fought the American soldiers. America might have lost the war.* DOK 3
2. *The author wants to describe an important event in history. The illustrator wants to show the event in a fun way by making the characters look like gingerbread men.* DOK 3
3. *At first, George Washington notices that the baker is fat and old. Then he notices that the baker is brave when he goes to talk to the soldiers. I think he learned not to judge people by how they look.* DOK 2

Cite Text Evidence

Write a Conversation

PROMPT How do you think General Washington reacted when the baker explained what happened with the hired soldiers? Use details from the text and pictures to explain your ideas.

PLAN First, draw a picture of the baker talking to General Washington. Show how each character feels. Add speech balloons to show what they are saying.

78

Write About Reading

- **Read aloud** the prompt.
- **Lead a discussion** in which children share their ideas about George Washington's reaction when the baker told him he convinced the German soldiers not to fight against the Americans. Tell them to use details in the text and pictures to support their ideas.
- Then read aloud the Plan section. Have children use ideas from the discussion to help them with their drawings.

DOK 3

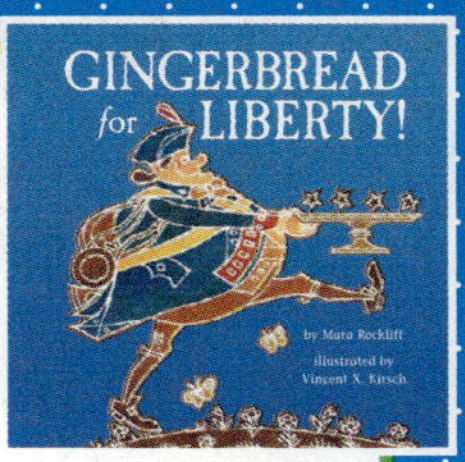

WRITE Now write a conversation between the baker and General Washington. Have the baker explain how he talked the hired soldiers out of fighting. Remember to:

- Look for details in the text that give clues about how General Washington might react.
- Include feeling words such as *amazed, proud, scared,* and *thrilled* to help the characters express how they feel.

Responses will vary.

79

Write About Reading

- **Read aloud** the Write section.
- **Encourage children** to include feeling words in their conversations to show the emotions Washington and the baker feel as they talk.

DOK 3

Independent Close Reading

Have children close read and annotate "An American Hero" on their own during small-group or independent work time. As needed, **use the Scaffolded Support notes** that follow to guide children who need additional help.

Scaffolded Support

As needed, remind children to:

- synthesize text details to figure out why the text is important.
- look for clues that help them understand how the text is organized, and think about how the organization helps them understand the author's ideas and purpose.

DOK 2

Prepare to Read

GENRE STUDY **Biographies** tell about real people's lives.

MAKE A PREDICTION Preview "An American Hero." Eleanor Roosevelt liked to help people. What do you think you will learn from reading this text?

I think I will learn what makes Eleanor Roosevelt an American hero.

SET A PURPOSE Read to find out why Eleanor Roosevelt is an important person in history.

An American Hero

READ As you read, think about what happened first, next, and last.

Eleanor Roosevelt was born in New York City in 1884. She was shy when she was little. When she was fifteen, she went to a boarding school in England. She was scared, but a kind teacher helped her. Soon Eleanor overcame her shyness.

In 1905, Eleanor married Franklin Roosevelt. Not long after, Franklin went into politics. Soon Eleanor began speaking up for things that were important to her, too.

Close Reading Tip

Write **C** when you make a connection.

Scaffolded Support

As needed, remind children to:

- circle words or phrases that help them understand the order in which the events happened.
- find ways that events or people described in the text remind them of their own life or of other texts they have read.

DOK 2

CHECK MY UNDERSTANDING

Which clues in the text tell you how the events are ordered?

The author gives dates and tells Eleanor's age.

READ As you read, answer the question, "What does this all mean to me?"

Then Franklin became president. Eleanor worked hard as the first lady. During wartime, Eleanor helped tend to the sick and hurt soldiers. She spoke out for all people in America to have the same rights. She also helped set rules for how people around the world should be treated. She thought this work was the best thing she did.

Sadly, Eleanor died in 1962. She will always be remembered for the change she brought to the world.

Close Reading Tip

Number the main events in order.

Scaffolded Support

As needed, remind children to:

- keep track of the most important details in the text, and then think about what the ideas in the text mean to them.
- remember that people who are an important part of history usually change people's lives in some way through their actions.

DOK 2

CHECK MY UNDERSTANDING

Why do you think Eleanor Roosevelt's accomplishments are an important part of American history?

Because she worked hard for others. Her work changed the world.

Cite Text Evidence

WRITE ABOUT IT "An American Hero" tells what Eleanor Roosevelt did to help people around the world. What do you think people thought of Eleanor? Use details from the text to explain your answer.

People probably thought Eleanor was a good person because she helped so many people. She tried to get the same rights for all people. People probably thought she was kind because she helped soldiers who were hurt.

83

Scaffolded Support

As needed, guide children to use details from the text to help them explain how people felt about Eleanor Roosevelt and the way she helped others.

DOK 3

Guided Practice

READ FOR UNDERSTANDING

Introduce the Text

- **Read aloud** and discuss the information about the genre.
- **Guide children** to set a purpose for reading to practice retelling a story in their own words.
- **Provide information** about the author, Ofelia Dumas Lachtman.
- **Tell children** to look for and think about the Power Words as they read.

Prepare to Read

GENRE STUDY **Realistic fiction** stories are made up but could happen in real life. As you read *Pepita and the Bully,* look for:

- characters who act and talk like real people
- events that could really happen
- setting in modern time in a place that could be real

SET A PURPOSE As you read, **retell** the story. Use your own words to tell what happened in the beginning, middle, and end of the story.

POWER WORDS

- wrinkled
- frown
- yanked
- dragged
- mumbled
- nearby
- excuses
- hesitant

Meet Ofelia Dumas Lachtman.

84

Pepita and the Bully

by Ofelia Dumas Lachtman
illustrated by Alex Pardo DeLange

READ FOR UNDERSTANDING

Make Predictions

- **Page through** the beginning of *Pepita and the Bully* with children.
- Have them **use prior knowledge, characteristics of the genre,** and the pictures to predict what the story will be about. Tell children they will **return to their predictions** after they finish reading the story.

DOK 2

Pepita waved goodbye to the bus driver. She raced down Pepper Street, her black braids bouncing behind her. She was in a hurry to get home and talk to Mamá. She wanted to tell her that three days in her new school were enough. She did not want to go there again.

86

READ FOR UNDERSTANDING

ASK: Who is the story's main character? *(Pepita)* **What do you learn about her from details in the words and pictures?** *(She has long black braids. She goes to a new school. She takes the bus there.)*

FOLLOW-UP: What problem does Pepita have? *(She does not like her new school. She doesn't want to go back.)*

DOK 2

Pepita's face wrinkled up into a big frown. She was sorry because she really liked Miss Chu, her teacher. Miss Chu had black eyes and a soft, sunny smile. Pepita also liked her classroom with bright bulletin boards and cut-out, red letters that said, "Welcome to a New School Year." She especially liked the playground with its tall shady tree and benches. But she did not like Babette. She had brown hair, blue eyes, and skin that looked like peach ice cream, but she was not nice.

87

 **READ FOR UNDERSTANDING**

Phonics/Decoding in Context

Have children point to the words *Chu, teacher*, and *peach*. Remind children that when the consonants *c* and *h* appear together in a word, they make one sound. Pronounce the *ch* sound; then point out the sound at the beginning, middle, or end of each of the words. **Guide children to blend** the letters and say each word.

 **READ FOR UNDERSTANDING**

ASK: What does Pepita like about school? What doesn't she like? Look for evidence that tells you. *(She likes her teacher Mrs. Chu, the classroom, and the playground. She doesn't like Babette because Babette is not nice.)*

DOK 2

TARGETED CLOSE READ

Theme

Have children reread pages 88–90 to analyze theme.

ASK: What is this story mostly about? *(It is about how Pepita deals with a bully.)* **What details in this part of the story help you identify the topic?** *(Babette is mean to Pepita and makes her feel sad and upset. Pepita does not want to go back to school because Babette is bullying her.)*

FOLLOW-UP: As you continue to read, what details will you look for to help you figure out the story's theme? *(Possible responses: I will look for details that explain how Pepita solves her problem; details that tell how the characters change; details that help me answer the question: What lesson does the author want me to learn?)*

DOK 2

Pepita's frown grew bigger when she remembered her first day of school. She had gone up to Babette and said, "Hello, my name's Pepita. What's yours?"

"Pepita, yuck," Babette said. "That's not a name. That's nothing but a noise."

Pepita felt her face grow hot. She was angry. "It is so a name," she said, "and it's mine!"

Babette just turned and walked away.

On the second day, Miss Chu asked her students to talk about their favorite things. Pepita told them her dog Lobo could understand Spanish.

At recess, Babette said, "I'll bet your dog has fleas."

Pepita felt her face grow hot. She was angry. "He does not!" she cried.

Babette just turned and walked away.

READ FOR UNDERSTANDING

ASK: How does Babette make Pepita feel? Use details to explain. *(Babette makes Pepita feel angry. Her face grows hot. The illustration shows Pepita looking upset. Her arms are crossed.)*

FOLLOW-UP: Why do you think Babette turns and walks away? *(Possible response: She might not want to hear Pepita say mean things back to her.)*

DOK 2

 READ FOR UNDERSTANDING

Retell

MODEL RETELLING

THINK ALOUD *Now I understand why Pepita is so upset. Babette isn't being nice to her. Before I continue to read, I'm going to pause and ask myself: What has happened so far in the story? On the first day of school Babette tells Pepita she doesn't like her name. The second day Babette tells Pepita her dog has fleas. Today Babette tells Pepita her braids look like raggedy ropes.*

DOK 2

 READ FOR UNDERSTANDING

Quick Teach Words

As needed to support comprehension, briefly explain the meaning of *raggedy* in this context.

- Something that is *raggedy* is old, worn, or slightly broken.

And today was even worse. Babette yanked her braids and said, "Your braids look like two raggedy ropes. You should cut them off."

Pepita felt her face grow hot. She was really angry. "They are *not* ropes," she cried. "They're braids! And if you pull them again, I'll tell Miss Chu!"

Babette yelled, "Tattletale, tattletale," and turned and walked away.

Pepita was glad when the school day was over. *Yes*, she thought as she raced home, *three days are enough. I don't want to go to that school again.*

90

In the middle of the block, Pepita saw Mrs. Green digging in her garden.

"Hello, Mrs. Green," she said, "Can I ask you something? Do you think my name is funny?"

"Why no, Pepita," Mrs. Green answered. "Your name has a very lovely sound. It reminds me of bright little flowers."

Pepita nodded and smiled. "That's nice," she said. "Thank you, Mrs. Green."

READ FOR UNDERSTANDING

Retell

ANNOTATION TIP: Have children circle the words on pages 91–93 that tell where Pepita stops on her way home from school.

ASK: What is the first thing Pepita does on her way home from school? *(She asks Mrs. Green if she thinks Pepita's name is funny.)*

FOLLOW-UP: Why do you think Pepita asks Mrs. Green this question? *(Babette made fun of Pepita's name earlier. Now Pepita wants to see what Mrs. Green thinks of her name.)*

DOK 2

READ FOR UNDERSTANDING

ANNOTATION TIP: Have children underline where Pepita sees José.

ASK: Why do you think Pepita asks José if Lobo understands Spanish? *(Pepita asks because after she told the class that Lobo could understand Spanish, Babette said Lobo has fleas.)*

FOLLOW-UP: How do you know that José makes Pepita feel better? Look for details in the text. *(Pepita smiles and thanks José for saying that Lobo understands Spanish, so I know she was happy about what he said.)*

DOK 2

A few houses down the block, Pepita saw José, the mailman, stepping out of his truck.

"Hello, Señor José," she called. "Can I ask you something? Do you think Lobo understands Spanish?"

"Why, yes, Pepita, I do," the mailman answered. "I told him to sit. And when he did, I said, '*Buen perrito*. Good little dog,' and he wagged and wagged his tail. Of course he understands Spanish."

Pepita nodded and smiled. "I thought so, too," she said. "Thank you, Señor José."

92

When Pepita was near her own house, she saw Mrs. Becker standing by her easel, painting a pot of red geraniums.

"Hello, Mrs. Becker," she said. "Can I ask you something? Do you think my braids look like raggedy ropes?"

"Why, no, Pepita," Mrs. Becker answered. "Your braids are very lovely. They remind me of black satin ribbons shining in the sun."

Pepita nodded and smiled. "That's nice," she said. "Thank you, Mrs. Becker."

 **READ FOR UNDERSTANDING**

Retell

ANNOTATION TIP: Have children underline where Pepita sees Mrs. Becker.

ASK: Use your own words to retell what happens when Pepita stops to talk to people on the way home from school. *(Pepita stops to talk to people on her way home from school. In the middle of the block she asks Mrs. Green if her name is funny. She says no. A few houses down the block Pepita asks José if her dog understands Spanish. He says yes. Near her own house Pepita asks Mrs. Becker if her braids look like raggedy ropes. She says her braids are lovely.)*

FOLLOW-UP: Why do you think these events are important? *(They help Pepita know that the mean things Babette said to her are not true.)*

DOK 2

 READ FOR UNDERSTANDING

Phonics/Decoding in Context

Have children point to the words *that* and *thought*. Remind children that when the consonants *t* and *h* appear together in a word, they make a single sound that can be voiced or unvoiced. Pronounce *that* and *thought*, stressing the different sounds of *th*. **Guide children to blend** the letters and say each word.

 READ FOR UNDERSTANDING

ASK: What questions do you have about Pepita's problem and how she will solve it? *(Possible response: Will Papá agree with Mamá and say that Pepita has to go to school? If that happens, what will Pepita do if she sees Babette? Will she look for help from someone else?)*

DOK 2

When Pepita got home, she found her mother in the kitchen. "Mamá," she said, "I can't go back to that school again."

"Why?" Mamá asked. "I thought you liked your new school."

"So did I," Pepita said, "until I talked to Babette."

"And who is Babette?" Mamá asked.

"Babette is a bully," Pepita said. "She's mean to me, Mamá. I'm not going back to school."

"No, no," Mamá said, "that cannot be. School is important. But let's see what Papá has to say."

94

At supper that night, Pepita told her family what Babette had said to her. "She says my name is nothing but noise, that Lobo has fleas, and that my braids are raggedy ropes. And she yanked them! That's why I'm not going back to school!"

"I see," Papá said, "but you have to go to school. So tomorrow if Babette yanks your braids again, you must tell your teacher. But if Babette says mean things to you, either you can answer her politely or you can walk away. But whatever you do, you must be kind."

"Kind?" Pepita asked. "Is that like *nice*?"

Papá nodded. "Yes, *nice* will do."

Pepita's brother Juan said, "Just don't fight with her. Bullies like fights."

 **READ FOR UNDERSTANDING**

Retell

ANNOTATION TIP: Have children identify and underline details that help them understand the advice Pepita gets from Mamá and Papá.

ASK: Retell the conversation Pepita has with Mamá and Papá in your own words. *(Mamá says that school is important and that Pepita has to go. Papá tells Pepita that when Babette is mean to her, she can choose to be polite or to walk away, but that she shouldn't fight with her.)*

DOK 2

 **READ FOR UNDERSTANDING**

ASK: Think back to your experience reading *Working with Others*. What advice do you think the author of that book would give Pepita? *(Possible response: I think the author would tell Pepita to work out her conflict with Babette peacefully. The author would say to talk to Babette nicely about the way she is acting.)*

DOK 4

READ FOR UNDERSTANDING

ANNOTATION TIP: Have children underline words and phrases that reveal how Pepita is feeling.

ASK: How does Pepita feel? Use evidence from the text to explain. *(Pepita is worried about what will happen if Babette bullies her again. She tosses and turns. She tells Dora that Babette will say mean things to her. She punches the pillow and wonders if Babette might hit her.)*

FOLLOW-UP: Do you think Dora's face really looks sad? Why do you think the narrator says this? *(Dora does not look sad in the illustration. I think it is how Pepita sees her. She imagines that Dora is sad because she is sad herself.)*

DOK 3

READ FOR UNDERSTANDING

Quick Teach Words

As needed to support comprehension, briefly explain the meaning of *tangle* in this context.

- Something that is in a *tangle* is all twisted up.

In bed Pepita tossed and turned and tumbled until her blankets were in a tangle. She dragged her doll Dora out from under the blankets and placed her against the pillow. "Dora," she said, "tomorrow Babette will say mean things to me."

Dora's face looked sad.

Pepita sat up straight and punched the pillow. "What if she tries to hit me?!"

Dora disappeared under the blankets.

Pepita pulled her out again. "Don't worry, Dora," she said, "I'll think of something." Dora huddled close. They snuggled together and fell asleep.

96

In the morning, Pepita got out of bed slowly. She dressed slowly. She ate breakfast slowly. She twisted and turned and muttered and mumbled while Mamá brushed and braided her hair. But no matter what Pepita did, nothing slowed down the clock. It was time to go to school.

"Mamá," Pepita complained, "three days are enough."

But Mamá said, "School is important, and if you don't hurry, you'll be late."

 **READ FOR UNDERSTANDING**

ASK: Why is Pepita doing everything slowly? *(She doesn't want to go to school because she is worried about what might happen with Babette. She is trying to delay having to go for as long as she can.)*

DOK 2

So Pepita went to school. Her classroom was sunny and bright. Her teacher smiled at her. But across the room Babette wrinkled up her nose and made an ugly face. At recess Mindy asked Pepita to play hopscotch. Pepita was about to say yes, but she saw Babette standing nearby. She gave Mindy a friendly wave, went to the farthest corner of the playground and sat under the shady tree. Babette was right behind her.

READ FOR UNDERSTANDING

ASK: Why do you think Pepita decides not to play with Mindy? *(Babette is standing nearby. I think Pepita is afraid that if she plays with Mindy, Babette will be mean to her in front of Mindy—or she might be mean to both of them.)*

DOK 2

"That's my bench," Babette said. "I don't like you sitting there."

Pepita stood up. "What *do* you like?" she asked, and started to walk away.

"I don't like you for sure," Babette said.

99

TARGETED CLOSE READ

Theme

Have children reread pages 99–102 to analyze the story's theme.

ASK: What does Pepita realize after she says something mean to Babette? *(She realizes that Papá's advice was right. It is better to be kind when someone is mean to you.)* **How does this affect the way she tells Babette how she feels about her being a bully?** *(She talks to Babette nicely, but she is also honest with her. She tells Babette that more kids would want to play with her if she wasn't so mean.)*

FOLLOW-UP: What theme, or big idea, do these details help you figure out? *(Possible response: How you treat others can help you make or lose friends.)*

DOK 3

Notice & Note

Contrasts and Contradictions

- **Remind children** that when characters act in a way that is unexpected, they should stop to notice and note. Retelling the events that led to the surprising action can help them understand an important idea.
- **Have children** explain why they might use this strategy on page 100. *(Babette cries when Pepita finally stands up to her, even though Babette has been the bully all along.)*

ANNOTATION TIP: Have children underline the words Pepita says that lead to Babette's surprising reaction.

- **Remind them** of the Anchor Question: **Why would the character act this way?** *(I think Babette doesn't really like herself. That is why she is a bully. When Pepita says something mean to her, she feels bad, just like Pepita did when Babette bullied her before.)*

DOK 3

Pepita felt her face grow hot. She was angry. She stopped and turned. "Maybe you don't like anything at all," she called.

"Maybe you don't even like your name. *Maybe you don't even like yourself.* And I'll bet you don't even have a dog!"

"You aren't nice," Babette said, and a tear rolled down her cheek. "You aren't nice at all."

100

Pepita's mouth dropped wide open. Her brother had told her not to fight. Papá had told her to be kind. And look what she had done! Babette was crying!

"Most times I'm nice," Pepita said, "and I'm polite, too. But you say mean things. Maybe if you stop being mean, somebody would ask you to play, too."

"I wouldn't play if you were playing because I don't like your braids," Babette said.

"See? You're being mean."

"I wouldn't play if you were playing because you have a funny name," Babette said.

"You're just being mean again. Anyway, Pepita's who I am."

101

 **READ FOR UNDERSTANDING**

Retell

ANNOTATION TIP: Have children underline important details that tell what happens when Pepita confronts Babette.

ASK: In your own words, retell what happens when Pepita finally stands up to Babette. *(When Babette tells Pepita that she can't sit on the bench, Pepita gets really mad. She says mean things and makes Babette cry. That makes Pepita feel bad. She tells Babette that people would ask her to play sometimes if she'd just stop being mean.)*

DOK 2

READ FOR UNDERSTANDING

Retell

MODEL RETELLING

THINK ALOUD *To retell the story, I will think about what happened in the beginning, the middle, and the end. Pepita goes to a new school. A girl named Babette is mean to her and makes her angry. On the way home on the third day, Pepita asks her neighbors questions. When she gets home, she tells her mother she doesn't want to go back to school because Babette is a bully. That night Pepita's parents explain that school is important and give her advice. At the end, Pepita finally stands up to Babette. She helps Babette see that more people will like her if she's nice. Finally, she and Babette become friends.*

DOK 2

READ FOR UNDERSTANDING

Wrap Up

Revisit the predictions children made before reading. Have them confirm or correct their predictions using evidence from the text and pictures.

DOK 2

"But I might play," Babette said, "if . . ."

"Stop making excuses!" Pepita said. "Do you want to play or don't you?"

Babette bit her lip, sniffed and gave a hesitant little nod.

"Okay," Pepita said, "but you'd better blow your nose."

She handed Babette a tissue from her pocket. Then she swung around and raced toward the center of the yard. "Wait, Mindy! Wait for us! Babette and I want to play!"

102

Respond to Reading

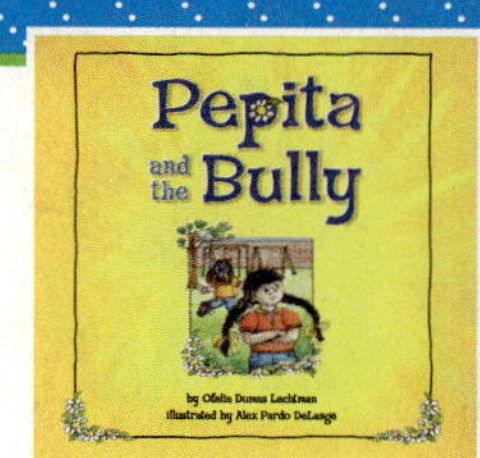

Use details from *Pepita and the Bully* to answer these questions with a partner.

1. **Retell** Take turns telling the story events in order. Use order words such as *first, next, after,* and *at the end* to help you.
2. Who is telling the story? Why do you think the author chose this point of view?
3. Papá tells Pepita to be kind. What do you think of this advice? Find details in the text and pictures that show how Pepita feels about it.

Talking Tip

Ask to learn more about one of your partner's ideas. Complete the sentence below.

Please tell me more about _____.

Academic Discussion

Use the TURN AND TALK routine. Remind children to follow agreed-upon rules for discussion, such as remembering to speak clearly and at a pace that allows their partner to understand what they are saying.

Possible responses:

1. *Accept reasonable responses.* DOK 2
2. *A narrator who is not a character is telling the story. I think the author chose this point of view so the reader could learn about all the characters, not just what Pepita says about them.* DOK 3
3. *Possible response: I think it is good advice. When Pepita says something mean to Babette, she feels bad that it upsets Babette. When she says something kind, she and Babette become friends.* DOK 3

Cite Text Evidence

Write a Letter

PROMPT What should Babette say to apologize to Pepita? Look for details in the text and pictures that tell what Babette did and how it made Pepita feel.

PLAN First, write notes about the things Babette should apologize for.

I am sorry for . . .

104

Write About Reading

- **Read aloud** the prompt.
- **Lead a discussion** in which children share their ideas about Babette's actions and how they made Pepita feel and respond. Tell them to use evidence from the text and pictures to support their ideas.
- Then read aloud the Plan section. Have children use ideas from the discussion to complete the graphic organizer.

DOK 3

WRITE Now help Babette apologize! Write an apology letter from Babette to Pepita. Remember to:

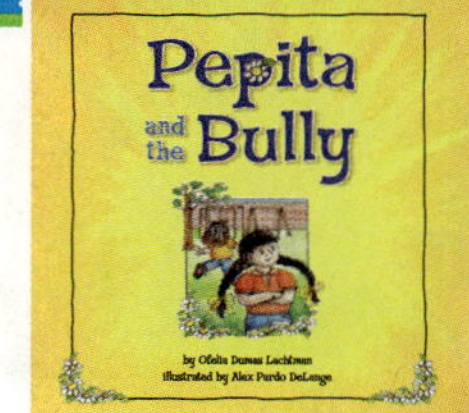

- Use the word *because* to explain why Babette is sorry.
- Begin your letter with *Dear Pepita*. End the letter with *Your friend, Babette.*

Responses will vary.

105

Write About Reading

- **Read aloud** the Write section.
- **Encourage children** to include signal words like *because* in their writing to help readers understand that a reason for an action is being described.
- **Remind children** that letters start with a greeting to the person receiving the letter and end with a signature from the person sending the letter.

DOK 3

Independent Close Reading

Have children close read and annotate "More Than One Way to Win" on their own during small-group or independent work time. As needed, **use the Scaffolded Support notes** that follow to guide children who need additional help.

Scaffolded Support

As needed, remind children to:

- check their understanding by using their own words to retell the important events in the order they happened.
- identify clues that point to the story's theme, or lesson the author wants to share with readers.

DOK 2

Prepare to Read

GENRE STUDY **Realistic fiction** stories are made up but could happen in real life.

MAKE A PREDICTION Preview "More Than One Way to Win." Alex and Maya are the fastest runners in the school. What do you think will happen when they have a disagreement?

I think they will solve their problem with a race.

SET A PURPOSE Read to find out what lesson the characters in the story learn.

106

More Than One Way to Win

READ What happens at the beginning of the story? Underline the reason Maya gets angry.

Maya and Alex are the fastest runners in school. They are friends, but they are always trying to beat each other on the track. One day, Maya hears Alex telling some friends that he just lets her win sometimes. Maya gets mad. She knows she shouldn't, but she says something mean to Alex. Now they aren't getting along. They decide to settle their disagreement with a race. ▶

Close Reading Tip

Number the main events in order.

CHECK MY UNDERSTANDING

What have you learned about Alex and Maya?

Alex and Maya are fast runners and friends.

107

Scaffolded Support

As needed, remind children that:

- at the beginning of a story, readers get to know the characters and learn more about the conflict, or problem they face.
- they can learn about characters in a story by paying attention to what the characters say, think, and do, as well as what other characters say and think about them.

DOK 2

READ What is this part of the story mostly about?

The race begins. Maya and Alex are tied the whole way. Then, Alex suddenly falls. Maya has to make a decision. Should she keep running or stop to help?

"I'm fine," Alex grunts, rubbing his ankle. "You go on."

"Don't be silly," Maya says as she pulls him up.

Then, leaning against each other, they hobble toward the finish line together.

Maya smiles. "I'm sorry we had a disagreement, Alex."

"I'm sorry, too. Maybe we should run relays together instead of racing against each other!" Alex suggests.

"Count me in. We make a great team!" Maya says.

Close Reading Tip

Put a **!** by a surprising part.

Scaffolded Support

As needed, guide children to:

- notice when characters do or say something you don't expect them to. Surprising moments can often point to a theme or lesson the author wants you to learn.
- look for a way that a character has changed from the beginning of the story to the end. Think about what the character learned that might have caused the change.

DOK 2

CHECK MY UNDERSTANDING

What lesson do Maya and Alex learn?

Working together is better than working against each other.

Cite Text Evidence

WRITE ABOUT IT Retell the story in your own words. Use details from the story to tell what happens in the beginning, the middle, and the end.

Maya and Alex aren't getting along. They decide to have a race to settle it. In the race, Alex falls down. Maya helps him up, and they finish the race together. They decide to find a race where they can work together instead of race against each other.

Scaffolded Support

As needed, remind children to stop after each event in the story and use their own words to describe what they learned. They can then connect their descriptions to retell the story's beginning, middle, and end.

DOK 2

READ FOR UNDERSTANDING

Introduce the Text

- **Read aloud** and discuss the information about the genre.
- **Guide children** to set a purpose for reading to practice identifying the central idea of an infographic in order to understand its purpose.
- **Provide information** about the background topic, bullying.

Guided Practice

Prepare to Read

GENRE STUDY **Infographics** give information quickly and in a visual way. As you read *Be a Hero! Work It Out!,* notice:

- the purpose of the infographic
- how pictures, symbols, and words work together
- words or phrases that stand out
- what the author wants you to learn

SET A PURPOSE Think about the infographic's **central idea.** How do the words, numbers, and symbols work together to help you understand the infographic's purpose?

Build Background: Bullying

110

by Ruben Cooley

Identify the problem.

Think about the problem.

Attack the problem, not the person.

Listen and have an open mind.

Be respectful of feelings.

Know that everyone makes mistakes—own up to yours.

Knock out these enemies:

Hitting Making threats Pushing Name-calling Making excuses Not listening Making mean faces Bullying

READ FOR UNDERSTANDING

Make Predictions

- **Page through** the beginning of *Be a Hero! Work It Out!* with children.
- Have them **use prior knowledge, characteristics of the genre,** and the pictures to predict what the text will be about. Tell children they will **return to their predictions** after they finish reading the text.

DOK 2

READ FOR UNDERSTANDING

Phonics/Decoding in Context

Have children point to the words *there* and *math*. Review the two pronunciations of the consonant digraph *th*. **Model pronunciation** of the words and the different sounds in *there* and *math*. Have children repeat. As needed, provide additional practice with the words *with* and *other*.

READ FOR UNDERSTANDING

Central Idea

ASK: What does Captain Problem Solver want you to do? *(Spread tips about how to solve problems.)*

FOLLOW-UP: Why do you think the author has a superhero give tips about the topic of the infographic? *(Possible responses: Kids like superheroes, so they will want to pay attention to what a superhero has to say. You will be a hero if you help others work out problems.)*

DOK 3

Hello, citizens!

Captain Problem Solver here!

I have been told there are some problems on the streets. Some kids don't know how to solve problems. No, not *math* problems—problems with each other. I need your help spreading the word about my tips!

SCHOOL

112

Let's break these down a little. When you are sharing my tips, these are three important ones to start with. When there is a problem, kids should first identify that there is a problem. People don't agree all the time. So they should think about what the problem is before doing anything. Remember to attack the problem, not the person. That would just make the problem worse!

READ FOR UNDERSTANDING

Central Idea

ASK: Why is it important to share these three tips first? *(The tips help you get started. You need to know what the problem is first, before you can solve it.)*

DOK 2

READ FOR UNDERSTANDING

ASK: What is the purpose of the numbered list? *(The list summarizes the information in the paragraph. The numbered steps make it easier to remember what to do.)*

ANNOTATION TIP: Have children circle the symbols before each number.

FOLLOW-UP: Why do you think the author includes a symbol for each tip? *(Possible response: They give a clue about what to do. For example, the magnifying glass tells you to look closely at the problem.)*

DOK 2

READ FOR UNDERSTANDING

Central Idea

ASK: What do the tips on this page help you understand? Why are these tips important? *(These tips explain what to do when trying to solve a problem; it is easier to solve a problem when you keep an open mind and are respectful of others' feelings.)*

FOLLOW-UP: How do these tips connect to the tips on page 113? *(The tips on page 113 tell how to identify the problem. The tips on page 114 tell you how to work with someone to solve the problem.)*

DOK 3

So what can kids do? Share the next three tips!

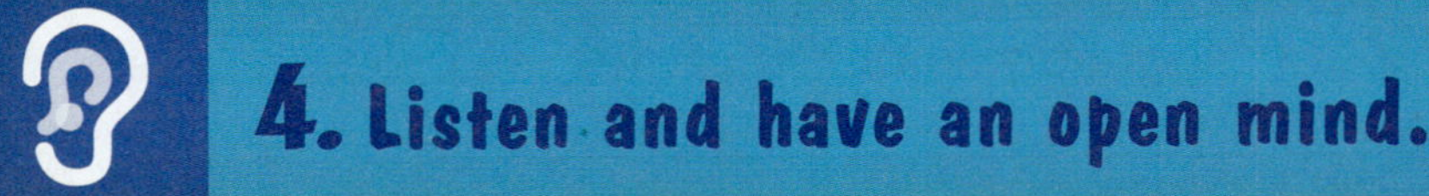

5. Be respectful of feelings.

6. Know that everyone makes mistakes—own up to yours.

Kids should listen to each other. Someone else might have a different idea of what happened. It could be just a misunderstanding. Listening to each other also shows that the other person's feelings are being respected. Knowing someone cares about your feelings makes you feel better, right? It can help with problem solving, too!

Finally, owning up to mistakes is part of life. As you share my tips with other kids, make sure you know this one well. Practice it yourself! Everyone can make mistakes, and admitting you have made one can be hard. It makes you a brave citizen to admit you have made one!

115

Notice & Note

Extreme or Absolute Language

- **Remind children** that when an author uses strong, forceful words to make a point, they should stop to notice and note how the author might be using the words to share his or her feelings about the topic.
- **Have children** explain why they might use this strategy on p. 115. *(The author tells me that I should practice owning up to mistakes. He must think this is a very important problem-solving skill to have, since he wants me to practice doing it.)*

ANNOTATION TIP: Have children underline words and phrases and circle punctuation that reflect strong, forceful language.

- **Remind them** of the Anchor Question: **What does this make me wonder about?** *(I wonder why the author put this tip last, if he thinks it's that important.)*

DOK 3

 READ FOR UNDERSTANDING

Central Idea

ASK: How do the words and phrases at the top of the page add to your understanding of the topic? *(They are actions that make problems worse. They tell what you should not do if you want to solve a problem in a peaceful way.)*

FOLLOW-UP: What is the central idea of this text? *(We can solve problems with others by thinking and following simple tips.)*

DOK 2

 READ FOR UNDERSTANDING

Wrap Up

Revisit the predictions children made before reading. Have them confirm or correct their predictions using evidence from the text and pictures.

DOK 2

These are the enemies that can stop kids from solving a problem and make the problem worse. Look for them every day and help stop them!

My work here is done. Thank you for sharing my tips about problem solving, citizens! I know with your help, we will have more citizens on the streets being problem solvers!

Be a problem solver superhero like me!

Respond to Reading

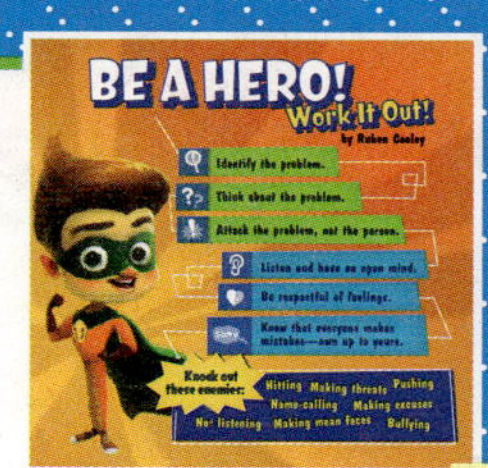

Use details from *Be a Hero! Work It Out!* to answer these questions with a partner.

1. **Central Idea** What is the hero's message? Which details in the text help you figure out the central idea?

2. How do the numbers, symbols, and words help you understand what the hero is trying to persuade you to do?

3. The hero says that it is brave to own up to your mistakes. Think about a time you made a mistake. How does that help you understand what the hero means?

Talking Tip

Complete the sentence to ask your partner for more information about an answer.

Tell me more about ___________.

Academic Discussion

Use the TURN AND TALK routine. Remind children to follow agreed-upon rules for discussions, such as waiting until their partner has finished speaking before adding a comment or thought.

Possible responses:

1. *The hero's message is that you can follow steps to find peaceful ways to solve problems. The steps on the first page help me figure out the central idea.* DOK 2
2. *Together, the numbers, symbols, and words help me understand how to follow the steps to solving a problem. The numbers tell me what order to follow them. The symbols help me understand what the steps are about. The words tell me what to do.* DOK 3
3. *Answers will vary.* DOK 4

Module Wrap-Up

Revisit the Essential Question

- **Read aloud** the Essential Question.
- **Remind children** that in this module, they read different texts about solving problems that can help them answer the question.
- **Have children** choose one of the activities to show what they learned in this module.

Sing It Out

- **Guide children** to brainstorm a list of words and phrases that describe helpful actions to take when solving a problem. Remind them that songs are a bit like poems. They often rhyme, but they don't need to.
- **Encourage children** to use the Big Idea Word *compromise* in their songs.
- **Invite children** to give their songs a unique melody and sing them for the class or create an audio recording of them.

DOK 3

Let's Wrap Up!

Essential Question

How can people work out disagreements?

Pick one of these activities to show what you have learned about the topic.

1. Sing It Out

Make up a song about what to do when a problem comes along. Look back at the texts for ideas about how to resolve a conflict. Share your song with the class.

Word Challenge

Can you use the word compromise in your song?

2. Make a Glossary

Find words in the texts that tell about solving problems. Make a list of at least five words. Then put them in ABC order. Write the meaning of each word next to the word.

My Notes

119

Make a Glossary

- **Guide children** to scan through the texts for relevant and appropriate words. Identify one or two and write them on the board so children know what they are looking for. Review the features of a glossary.
- **Encourage children** to look up each word in a print or digital student dictionary. Have them write a few words or draw a picture that shows the meaning of the word and include the definition in their glossaries.

DOK 3

Brainstorm and Plan

- **Have children** use the My Notes space to jot down ideas for their chosen activity. Remind them to refer back to their notes as they complete the activity.

Introduce the Topic

- **Read aloud** the module title, *Once Upon a Time*.
- **Tell children** that in this module they will be reading texts about the topic of storytelling.
- **Have children** share prior knowledge about the topic or word associations for storytelling. Record their ideas in a web.

Discuss the Quotation

- **Read aloud** the quotation by Roald Dahl.
- **Lead a discussion** in which children try to explain the quote in their own words. Explain the meaning, as needed: *When we read a book we love, we continue to think back on it because we learn a lot about the characters and begin to care about them as much as we do our own friends.*

ASK: Who are some of your favorite storybook characters? What do you like about them? *(Accept reasonable responses.)*

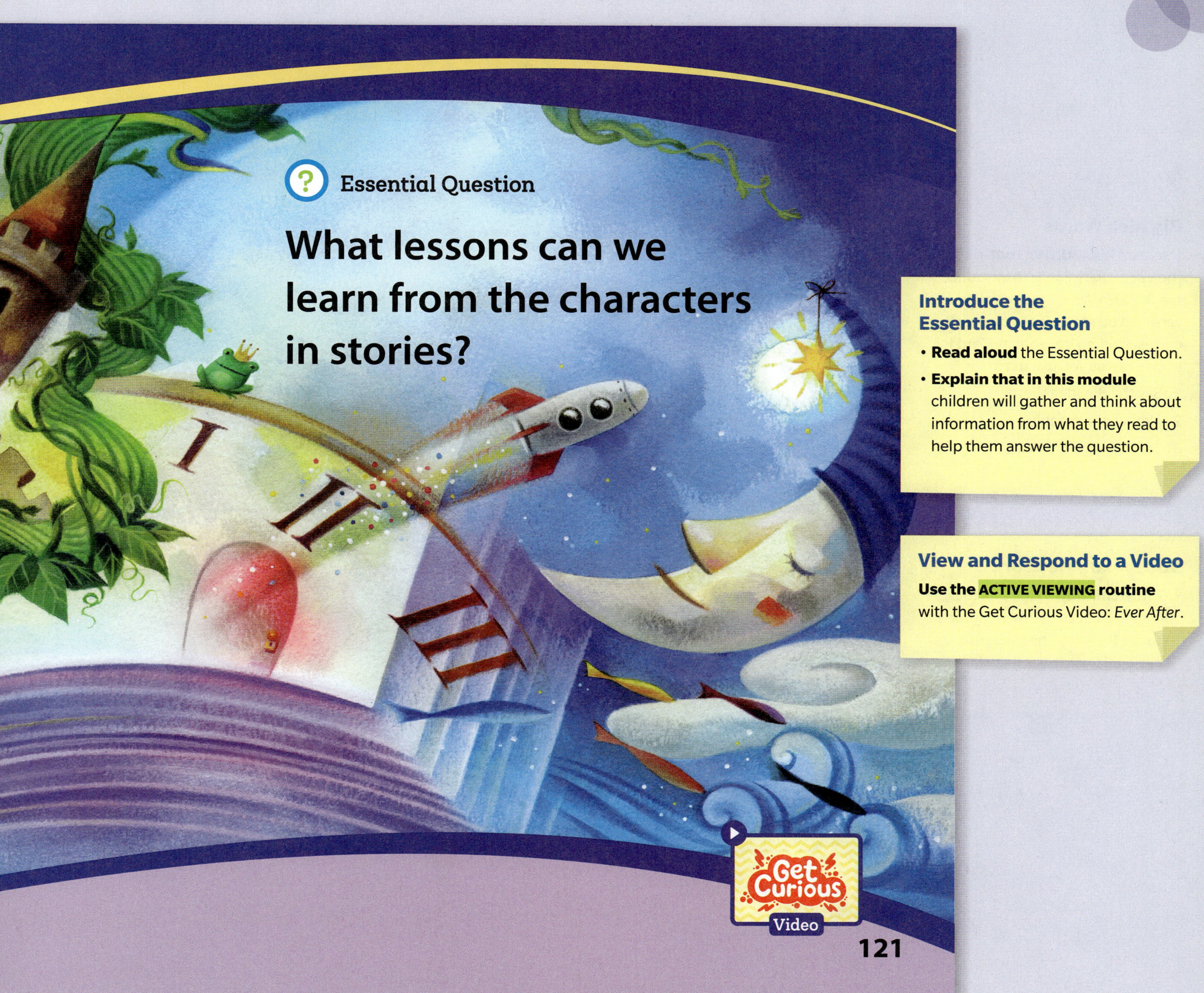

Introduce the Essential Question

- **Read aloud** the Essential Question.
- **Explain that in this module** children will gather and think about information from what they read to help them answer the question.

View and Respond to a Video

Use the ACTIVE VIEWING routine with the Get Curious Video: *Ever After*.

Big Idea Words

Use the VOCABULARY routine and the Vocabulary Cards to introduce the Big Idea Words *moral, relate,* and *version*. You may wish to display the corresponding Vocabulary Card for each word as you discuss it.

1. Say the Big Idea Word.
2. Explain the meaning.
3. Talk about examples.

Vocabulary Network

- **Guide children** to think of the lessons characters have learned in stories they have heard or read as they complete the activity for *moral*.

Big Idea Words

Words About Storytelling

Complete the Vocabulary Network to show what you know about the words.

moral	
Meaning: A **moral** is a lesson in a story.	
Synonyms and Antonyms	**Drawing**

relate

Meaning: If you **relate** to someone, you know how the person feels.

Synonyms and Antonyms	Drawing

version

Meaning: A **version** is a different or changed form of something.

Synonyms and Antonyms	Drawing

Vocabulary Network

- **As children complete** the activity for *relate,* encourage them to draw a picture of an action they might take to show a friend that they understand how he or she feels.
- **Tell children** they may want to draw two pictures to illustrate the word *version,* one to show the original item and another to show a different form of it.

READ FOR UNDERSTANDING

Introduce the Text

- **Read aloud** the title, *Recipe for a Fairy Tale*. Tell children that it is a recipe. Ask them to share what they know about recipes. *(They are instructions for making food or other items.)*
- Guide children to **set a purpose.**
- **Read the text** with children.

DOK 2

READ FOR UNDERSTANDING

Text Organization

ASK: Why did the author write this recipe? *(to show people how to make a fairy tale)*

ANNOTATION TIP: Have children circle the numbers of the steps in the directions.

FOLLOW-UP: How are the directions organized? *(They are divided into steps. The steps are in chronological order.)* **Why do you think the author organized the directions this way?** *(The organization makes it easy to know when to do each step so the recipe turns out properly.)*

DOK 2

Short Read

Recipe for a Fairy Tale

You can use a recipe to make breakfast, lunch, or dinner. Can you use one to make a fairy tale, too? Let's find out!

Ingredients

prince

princess

dragon

castle

golden eggs

picnic basket

Directions

1. First, let's do some mixing.
2. Take the castle and the dragon.
3. Add a prince, a princess, and a picnic basket.
4. Now, sprinkle in a little bit of silliness.
5. Stir them all together. What have you got? Read on to find out!

The Story

Once upon a time, a dragon lived all alone in a castle. He never came out or opened the door. The villagers thought he was mean.

One day, a brave prince and a daring princess decided to save their frightened kingdom from the dragon. They marched up to the castle door. The prince hollered, "Open this door, or I'll huff and puff and blow your house down!"

The dragon was very surprised. He peeked out a window and asked, "Really? What if I **do** open the door?"

The princess held up a picnic basket. "Then we can have lunch," she said.

The lonely dragon opened the door. He invited his new friends in for lunch. They all lived happily ever after.

Be the Chef!

What would you mix up for a fairy tale?

125

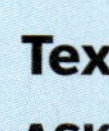

READ FOR UNDERSTANDING

Text Organization

ASK: Why did the author include this story with the recipe? *(The story is what you make when you follow the steps in the recipe correctly.)*

ANNOTATION TIP: Have children circle each ingredient from the recipe as they come across it in the story.

FOLLOW-UP: Suppose you were using the recipe to make a story. What would happen if you started with step 3 of the directions instead of step 1? *(The story would not make sense. It would start with the prince and princess instead of the castle and the dragon.)*

DOK 2

Guided Practice

Prepare to Read

GENRE STUDY **Procedural texts** tell readers how to do or make something. When you read *How to Read a Story*, notice:

- directions for readers to follow
- main topic and details
- steps that show order
- ways visuals and words help readers understand the text

SET A PURPOSE Read to make smart guesses, or **inferences,** about things the author does not say. Use clues in the text and pictures to help you.

POWER WORDS

cozy

steaming

clue

sense

pause

disturb

rattled

tackled

Meet Kate Messner.

126

READ FOR UNDERSTANDING

Introduce the Text

- **Read aloud** and discuss the information about the genre.
- **Guide children** to set a purpose for reading to practice making inferences.
- **Provide information** about the author, Kate Messner.
- **Tell children** to look for and think about the Power Words as they read.

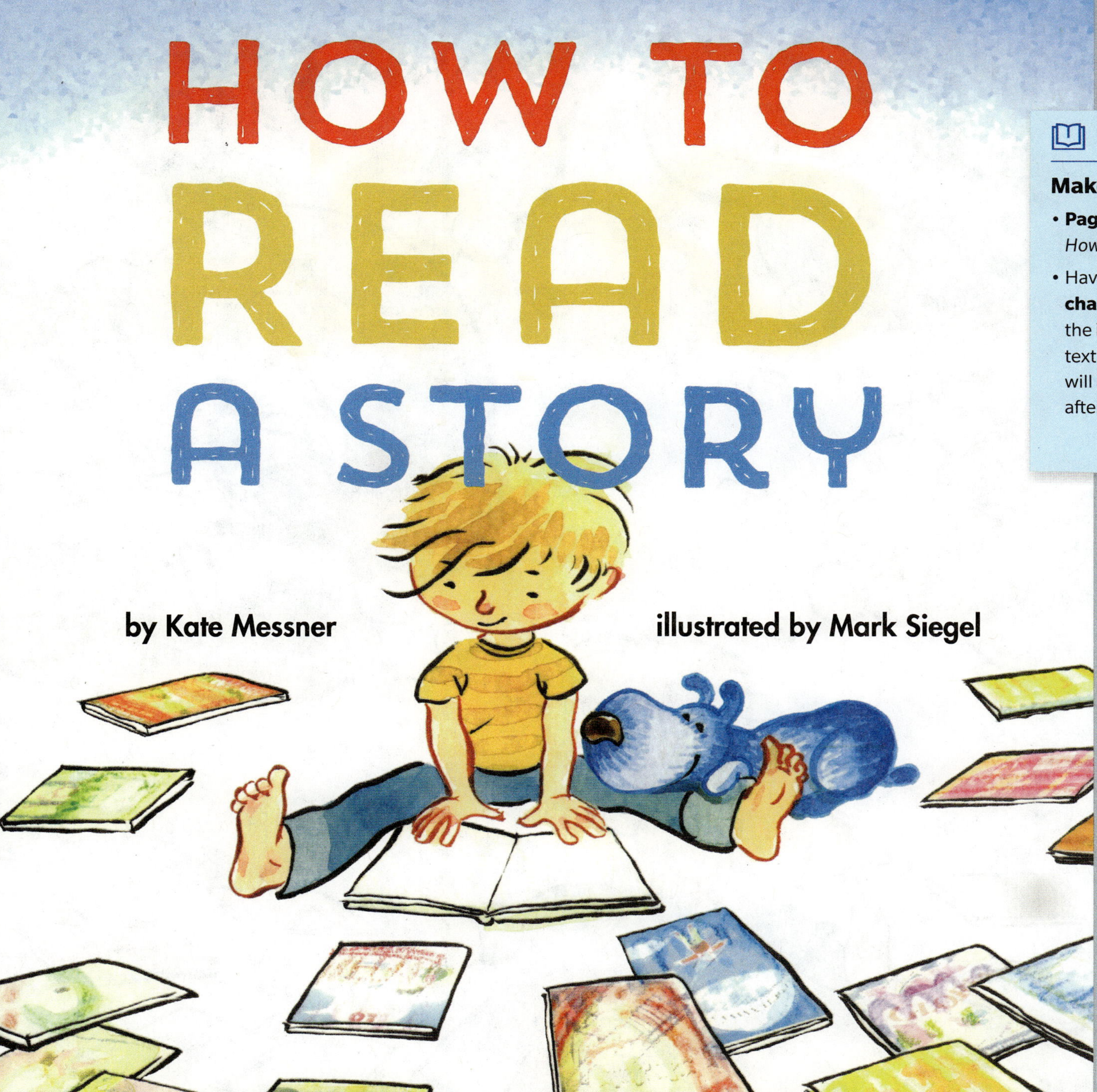

READ FOR UNDERSTANDING

Make Predictions

- **Page through** the beginning of *How to Read a Story* with children.
- Have them use **prior knowledge, characteristics of the genre,** and the illustrations to predict what the text will be about. Tell children they will **return to their predictions** after they finish reading the text.

DOK 2

READ FOR UNDERSTANDING

Make Inferences

MODEL MAKING AN INFERENCE

THINK ALOUD *I'm not sure what the boy is doing in this picture, so I'm going to look for details that will help me make a smart guess. The boy is surrounded by books. There are thought bubbles coming out of his head. He is thinking about all sorts of things, like green monsters, running pigs, and sword fights. I know that books can tell stories about all different kinds of characters. I think the boy is trying to pick out a book, and the books around him are about all the different characters he is thinking about.*

DOK 2

STEP 1

FIND A STORY.

A good one.
It can have princesses and castles,
if you like that sort of thing,
or witches and trolls.
(As long as they're not too scary.)

READ FOR UNDERSTANDING

ASK: Based on the text and the pictures, what questions do you have about why the author wrote the book? *(Possible responses: Why did the author write the book? Is she trying to inform or entertain?)*

DOK 2

TARGETED CLOSE READ

Text Organization

Have children reread pages 129–133 to analyze the text structure.

ANNOTATION TIP: Have children circle the step number and heading under each step.

ASK: What do you notice about how the book is organized? *(Each part is a step. The steps are in chronological order. A heading describes what is happening in each step.)*

FOLLOW-UP: How does the organization help you understand why the author wrote the book? *(It helps me understand that the author wrote the book to explain how to read a story. Each step gives information about what to do.)*

DOK 2

STEP 2

FIND A READING BUDDY.

A good one.

A buddy can be older . . .

or younger . . .

READ FOR UNDERSTANDING

Make Inferences

ASK: How is reading with an older reading buddy different from reading with a younger reading buddy? *(Possible response: An older reading buddy reads to you or can help you read; you read to a younger reading buddy.)*

FOLLOW-UP: Why do you think the author includes a dog in the illustration? Can a dog be a reading buddy? Explain why or why not. *(Many people have pets. The author is showing different examples of who or what can be a reading buddy. The boy could read to a baby or a dog.)*

DOK 2

or a person your age.

 **READ FOR UNDERSTANDING**

Make Inferences

ASK: What is the most important idea the author shares about a reading buddy? *(There are many different kinds of reading buddies.)*

FOLLOW-UP: Why should your reading buddy be nice and snuggly? *(Possible answers: It's more fun to read when you're snuggled up with someone! When you are reading with a buddy, you usually sit closely.)*

DOK 2

Or maybe not a person at all.

 **READ FOR UNDERSTANDING**

Phonics/Decoding in Context

Have children point to the word *back*. Say the word aloud; then review that /k/ is sometimes spelled with the letters *c* and *k*. Together the letters make one sound. The *ck* spelling can appear in the middle or at the end of a word, but never at the beginning. **Model blending** the sounds in the word: /b/ /ă/ /k/, *back*. Have children repeat.

Make sure your reading buddy is nice and snuggly.
And make sure you both like the book.
If you don't agree . . . go back to Step 1.
Sometimes it takes a few tries to find just the right book.

READ FOR UNDERSTANDING

Make Inferences

ASK: Do you think the boy and the dog have found a cozy spot to read? Explain with details from the text and the illustration. *(Possible response: Yes, the boy and the dog look very comfortable sitting on the chair close together reading a book. They are both wearing thick woolen hats that keep them warm. A woolen blanket and cup of steaming hot cocoa also make the boy feel cozy.)*

DOK 2

STEP 3

FIND A COZY READING SPOT.

Outside is fun . . . but not if it's very cold. Unless you have thick woolen blankets, and hats and scarves, and cups of steaming hot cocoa.

132

And not if it's very hot.
Unless you have trees to shade you from the sun, a hammock to catch cool breezes, and tall glasses of icy lemonade.

Inside is good.
Couches are cozy. So are chairs big enough for two.

Just be careful not to get stuck.

133

READ FOR UNDERSTANDING

ASK: What makes a reading spot cozy? Summarize with details from the text and illustration. *(It can be outside if you are dressed for the weather and have things to make you comfortable, like drinks. It can also be inside if you have a spot big enough for two.)*

DOK 2

READ FOR UNDERSTANDING

Phonics/Decoding in Context

Have children point to the word *stuck*. Say the word aloud; then review that the letters *ck* make the sound of /k/ when they appear together. **Model blending** the sounds in the word: /s/ /t/ /ŭ/ /k/, *stuck*. Have children repeat; then provide additional practice with the word *hammock*.

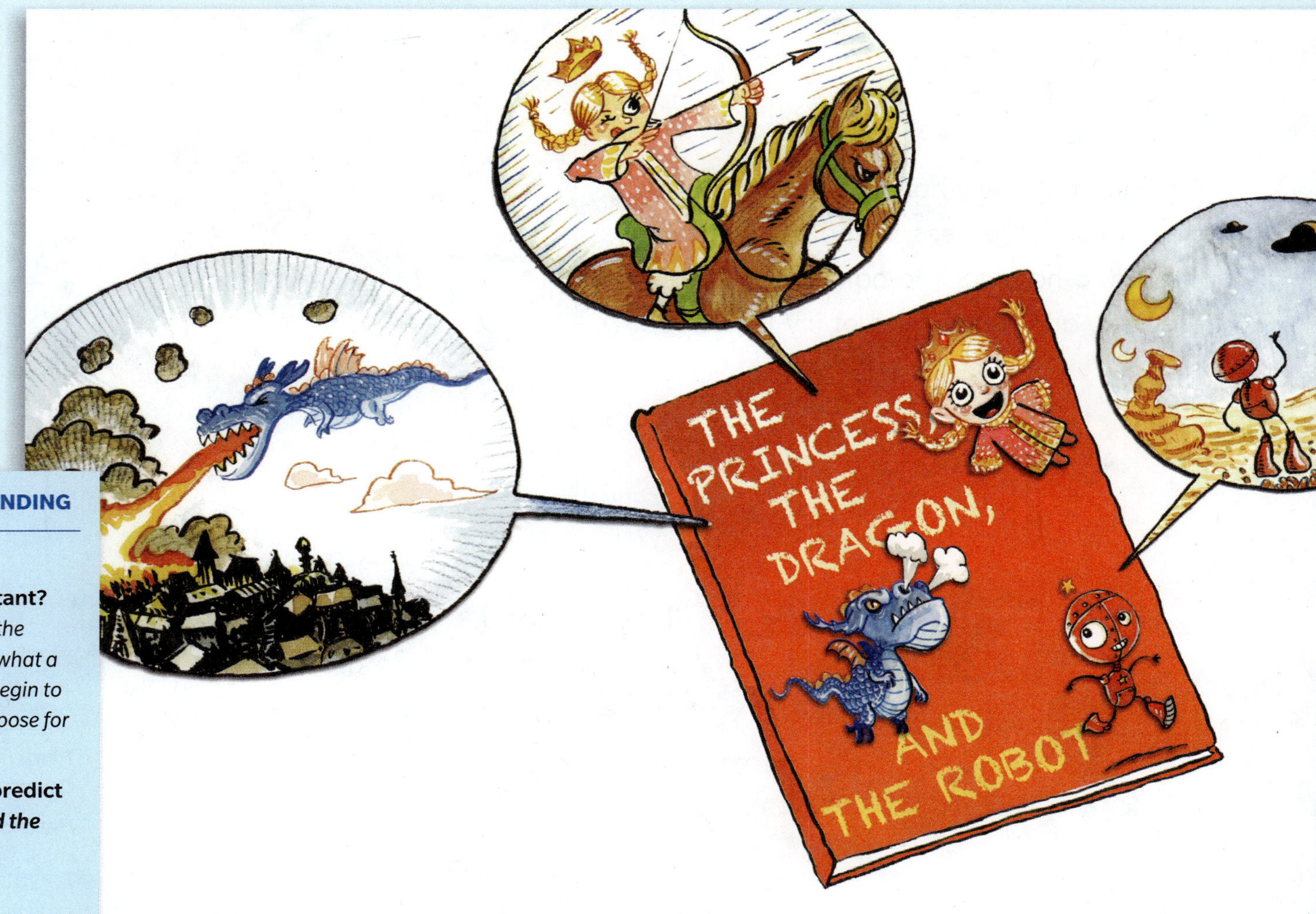

READ FOR UNDERSTANDING

Make Inferences

ASK: Why is this step important? *(Possible response: Looking at the book's cover helps you predict what a book will be about before you begin to read. It also helps you set a purpose for reading.)*

FOLLOW-UP: What do you predict *The Princess, the Dragon, and the Robot* will be about? *(Accept reasonable responses.)*

DOK 2

STEP 4

LOOK AT THE BOOK'S COVER.

Can you guess what it's about?
Read the title. That might be a clue.

STEP 5

OPEN THE BOOK.

(This is the exciting part!)

Read the story in a loud, clear voice, not too slow and not too fast.

You can point to words if you like, but you don't have to do that.

“Once upon

135

 **READ FOR UNDERSTANDING**

Make Inferences

ASK: Why do you think the author says that opening the book is “the exciting part”? *(When you first open the book, you don't know anything about the story. It is exciting to think about what the story will be like and what will happen to the characters.)*

FOLLOW-UP: Think about what you learn in this step. How does that help you understand why the words “Once upon a time” are part of the picture? *(Step 5 tells what to do when you open a book and begin the story. Many stories begin with those words, so they might be the first words you would read.)*

 **READ FOR UNDERSTANDING**

Quick Teach Words

As needed to support children's comprehension, briefly explain the meaning of *clear* in context.

- *Clear* can have different meanings. Speaking in a *clear* voice means speaking in a way that others can understand easily.

TARGETED CLOSE READ

Text Organization

Have children reread pages 136–139 to analyze how the chronological text structure contributes to the author's purpose.

ASK: Why do you think the author does not give a heading under each numbered step? *(Possible response: The information in these steps all fit under what you do after you open the book, which is the heading for Step 5.)*

FOLLOW-UP: What is the connection between the pictures here and the pictures on pages 134–135? *(Most of the illustrations give information about what is happening in the story the boy is reading. On page 135 the illustration shows the boy and his reading buddy.)* ***How do the illustrations give information about how to read a story?*** *(They give examples from a story that help you understand what good readers do.)*

DOK 3

When the characters talk,
whatever's being said . . .
say it in a voice to match who's talking.

"I will save the kingdom."

"I am the most POWERFUL in all the land!"

"I'm hungry for lunch."

"Soon the castle will be MINE."

"Beep."

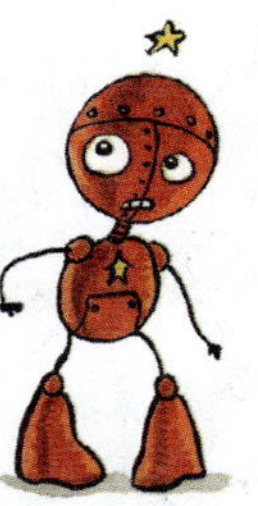

136

STEP 7

No matter what you read, hold the book so your buddy can see the pictures. Buddies get impatient when they can't see well.

STEP 8

If there are words you don't know, try sounding them out or looking at the pictures to see what makes sense.

"They were afraid the dragon would burn down the cass . . . cass . . . Oh . . . The castle!"

137

Notice & Note

Quoted Words

- **Remind children** that a quote is words said by a person other than the author. When children see a quote, they should stop to notice and note. Asking why the author chose to include the quote can help them better understand the text.
- **Have children** explain why they might use this strategy on page 137. *(There is a quotation on this page. Someone is trying to sound out the word* castle.*)*

ANNOTATION TIP: Have children circle the quotation marks around the quote.

- **Remind them** of the Anchor Question: **What does this make me wonder about?** *(I wonder who said this quotation. I know that Step 8 is about figuring out words you don't know. I think the boy reading the story is doing Step 8. He is sounding out* castle *to figure out what the word is.)*

DOK 3

If you need a break, you can pause for a minute . . .
and talk to your reading buddy
to predict what might happen next.

READ FOR UNDERSTANDING

Quick Teach Words

As needed to support children's comprehension, briefly explain the meaning of *break* in this context.

- *Break* can have many different meanings. Here, it is used as a noun. A *break* is a short rest or stop. After you take a *break*, you return to whatever it was you were doing.

138

Will the castle catch on fire?
Will the princess tame the dragon?
Will the robot marry the princess?
Will the horse make friends with the dragon?
Will the dragon eat them all for lunch?

139

READ FOR UNDERSTANDING

Make Inferences

ASK: What are the boy and the dog doing? *(They are taking a break and thinking about what might happen next.)* **What do the smaller pictures show?** *(They show the different predictions that the boy and the dog make on page 139.)*

ANNOTATION TIP: Have children draw lines from each illustration to the prediction that accompanies it.

FOLLOW-UP: Why is it important to talk to your reading buddy about what will happen next? *(Possible response: Each reader may make a different prediction. Talking about why you made a prediction may help your reading buddy notice different clues in the text and the illustrations.)*

DOK 2

READ FOR UNDERSTANDING

Make Inferences

MODEL MAKING INFERENCES

THINK ALOUD *In Step 9, the author says to make my voice sound exciting when I get to exciting parts of the story, but she doesn't really tell me how to do this. Let's see if I can figure out what she means. I think the text in the picture is from the story that the boy is reading. The princess has just captured the dragon! If I were the princess, I would sound very excited because I had just tackled the dragon. I think that's what the author means. She wants me to read the exciting parts in an excited way—like how the character would say them!*

DOK 2

READ FOR UNDERSTANDING

Quick Teach Words

As needed to support children's comprehension, briefly explain the meaning of *dares* in context.

- When a person *dares* to do something, they do it in a brave or courageous way.

STEP 9

When you get to the exciting parts, make your voice sound exciting, too.

"Who dares disturb me in my cave?" the dragon growled.

"Oh dear! Oh no!" The robot was so scared all his metal parts rattled. What would they do?

But the princess tackled that dragon and held him down.

"You must promise you'll leave our kingdom in peace!"

140

When you and your buddy can't stand it a second longer . . .

turn the page to read how things work out.

READ FOR UNDERSTANDING

ASK: Why do you think the information on this page is part of Step 9? *(Step 9 tells what to do during really exciting parts of the story. The information on this page explains that when the story is really exciting, you can turn the page and find out what happens next.)*

DOK 2

READ FOR UNDERSTANDING

ASK: What questions could you ask yourself about what you see in the illustration? *(Who are the people behind the boy? What are they doing?)*

FOLLOW-UP: What are the answers to your questions? *(They are the boy's other reading buddies. I think they are listening as the boy reads the most exciting part of the story out loud.)*

DOK 2

STEP 10

When the book is over, say,

READ FOR UNDERSTANDING

ASK: What questions do you have about the illustration on this page? *(Possible response: Who are the people in the illustration? Why are the people in the illustration cheering and clapping?)*

DOK 2

142

"The End."

READ FOR UNDERSTANDING

Make Inferences

ASK: How well did the boy follow the steps in the text? Use clues in the text and illustration to make an inference. *(I think the boy followed the steps just as the author described them. The words "they all lived happily ever after" in his book tell me that he reached the end of the story. His reading buddies are clapping, and he looks happy and excited. This makes me think he followed all the steps and had a fun time reading the story.)*

DOK 2

READ FOR UNDERSTANDING

ASK: Describe a time when you loved a story so much, you wanted to read it again right away. *(Accept reasonable responses.)*

FOLLOW-UP: How does connecting to that experience help you understand why the boy wants to read the story again? *(It made me think the story was so good, he didn't want it to end. When it did, he jumped right back into the story so he could enjoy it again.)*

DOK 4

READ FOR UNDERSTANDING

Wrap Up

Revisit the predictions children made before reading. Have them confirm or correct their predictions using evidence from the text and pictures.

DOK 2

And then . . . if it was a really good story . . .
go right back to the beginning
and start all over again.

144

Respond to Reading

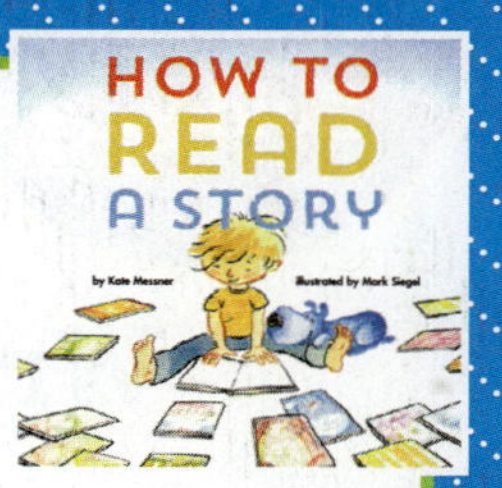

Use details from *How to Read a Story* to answer these questions with a partner.

1. **Make Inferences** Why is it important to find just the right book for you and your reading buddy?

2. How are the numbered steps in the text connected? What does the author want you to learn from them?

3. How do you think the author feels about reading? How do you think she wants others to feel about it? Use details from the text to explain your ideas.

Talking Tip

Your ideas are important! Be sure to speak loudly and clearly as you share them.

145

Academic Discussion

Use the TURN AND TALK routine. Remind children to follow agreed-upon rules for discussion, such as speaking loudly and clearly as they share ideas with one another.

Possible responses:

1. *Because the story should be about something you and your reading buddy like so that you will both enjoy it.* DOK 2
2. *The steps are in order to tell you how to read a story from beginning to end. The author wants you to learn how to read and enjoy a story.* DOK 2
3. *I think the author loves reading and wants others to love it, too. The steps in the text tell ways to make reading fun.* DOK 3

Cite Text Evidence

Write More Steps

PROMPT Think about how following the steps in *How to Read a Story* can help make reading fun. Now think about what makes reading fun for you. What other steps could you add to the text?

PLAN First, draw two steps that you would like to share with others. Be sure they are different from the steps in the text.

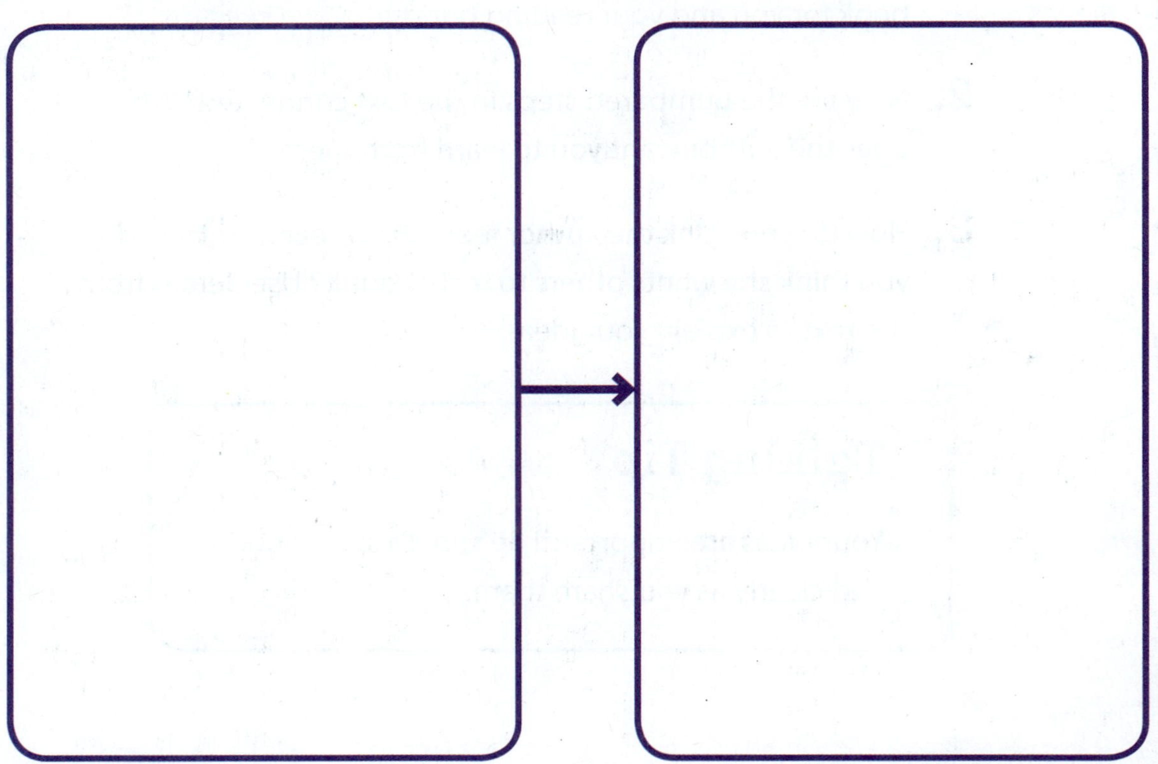

146

Write About Reading

- **Read aloud** the prompt.
- **Lead a discussion** in which children share their ideas about additional steps they could take to make reading fun. Remind them to use details from the text and illustrations to support their ideas.
- Then read aloud the Plan section. Have children use ideas from the discussion to help them with their drawings. Remind them that their ideas should be different in some way from the steps the author gave in the text.

DOK 3

WRITE Now write your own steps to add to *How to Read a Story*. Remember to:

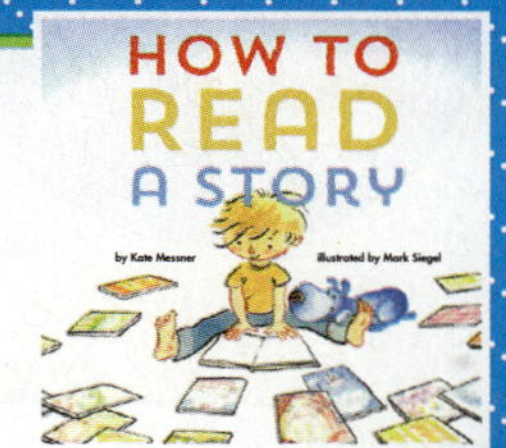

- Choose verbs that tell your readers exactly what to do.
- Use language that will make readers excited about following your steps.

Responses will vary.

Write About Reading

- **Read aloud** the Write section.
- **Encourage children** to choose verbs that tell the reader exactly what to do and use vivid descriptions to get readers interested and excited about reading a book.

DOK 3

On My Own

Independent Close Reading

Have children close read and annotate "How to Find a Story" on their own during small-group or independent work time. As needed, **use the Scaffolded Support notes** that follow to guide children who need additional help.

Scaffolded Support

As needed, remind children to:

- use information in the text along with what they already know to infer ideas the author doesn't tell them.
- look for clues that help them understand how the text is organized and think about how the organization helps them understand the author's ideas and purpose.

DOK 2

Prepare to Read

GENRE STUDY **Procedural texts** explain to readers how to make or do something.

MAKE A PREDICTION Preview "How to Find a Story." Look at the features, like the numbers and bold text. What do you think you will read about?

I think I will learn the steps for getting ideas for a story.

SET A PURPOSE Read to learn how to find a story and to see if your prediction is right. If not, think about the text and look carefully at the features. Then make a new prediction.

148

How to Find a Story

READ Why might beginning to write a story be a little scary?

What do all writers have in common? They all begin with a blank piece of paper. A blank piece of paper can be exciting! It is full of possibilities. Just think of all the stories that have come to life on a piece of paper. That blank paper can be a little bit scary, too. How is it going to be filled?

One way to get ideas is to read, read, READ. Most writers read a lot. They study how *their* favorite writers create characters and describe events. They think about the ingredients for a great story.

What other things can writers do to help them create?

Close Reading Tip

Write **C** when you make a connection.

149

Scaffolded Support

As needed, remind children that:

- underlining key ideas and events as they read will help them find evidence later when they want to answer a question or make an inference.
- connecting their own experiences with what they read can help them relate to the text.

DOK 2, 4

Close Reading Tip

Mark important ideas with *.

READ How are the steps in this list connected?

These steps will help you think of ideas to write about.

1. **Be curious!** Ideas are everywhere. Look and listen wherever you go.
2. **Write notes.** Keep a notebook with you. Write and make sketches about the ideas you find.
3. **Take risks!** An idea might seem wild or wacky now, but it can turn into something wonderful. Don't be afraid to make mistakes. That is how you learn!
4. **Write every day.** Use the ideas in your notebook. Maybe you write a little bit. Maybe you write a lot. See where your ideas take you.

When it's time to fill that blank page, you will be ready!

Scaffolded Support

As needed, remind children to:

- pay close attention to the way the steps in the list are organized and how one step is connected to the next.
- think about what the author is trying to explain in this part of the text and how the list helps the author do that.

DOK 2

CHECK MY UNDERSTANDING

What is the author's purpose for writing this text? Why does the author include a numbered list?

The author wants to help people think of story ideas. The numbered list tells what you can do to get ideas.

Cite Text Evidence

WRITE ABOUT IT Read the steps carefully. What other steps could help writers find and grow their ideas? Write two more steps that you would add to the author's list. Be sure to think about the order of the steps. Where do your new steps fit in?

Responses will vary.

151

Scaffolded Support

As needed, remind children to:

- use their notes and text markings to find evidence they can use to support the new steps they are adding to the process.
- add their ideas in the appropriate sequential order.

DOK 3

READ FOR UNDERSTANDING

Introduce the Text

- **Read aloud** and discuss the information about the genre.
- **Guide children** to set a purpose for reading to practice creating mental images.
- **Provide information** about the author, Crystal Hubbard.
- **Tell children** to look for and think about the Power Words as they read.

Guided Practice

Prepare to Read

GENRE STUDY **Dramas** are plays that are read and performed. As you read *A Crow, a Lion, and a Mouse! Oh, My!*, look for:

- the setting, or where and when the story takes place
- a narrator who reads words the characters do not say
- a list of characters

SET A PURPOSE As you read, **create mental images,** or make pictures in your mind, to help you understand details in the text.

POWER WORDS

- plain
- bind
- narrow
- clever

Meet Crystal Hubbard.

152

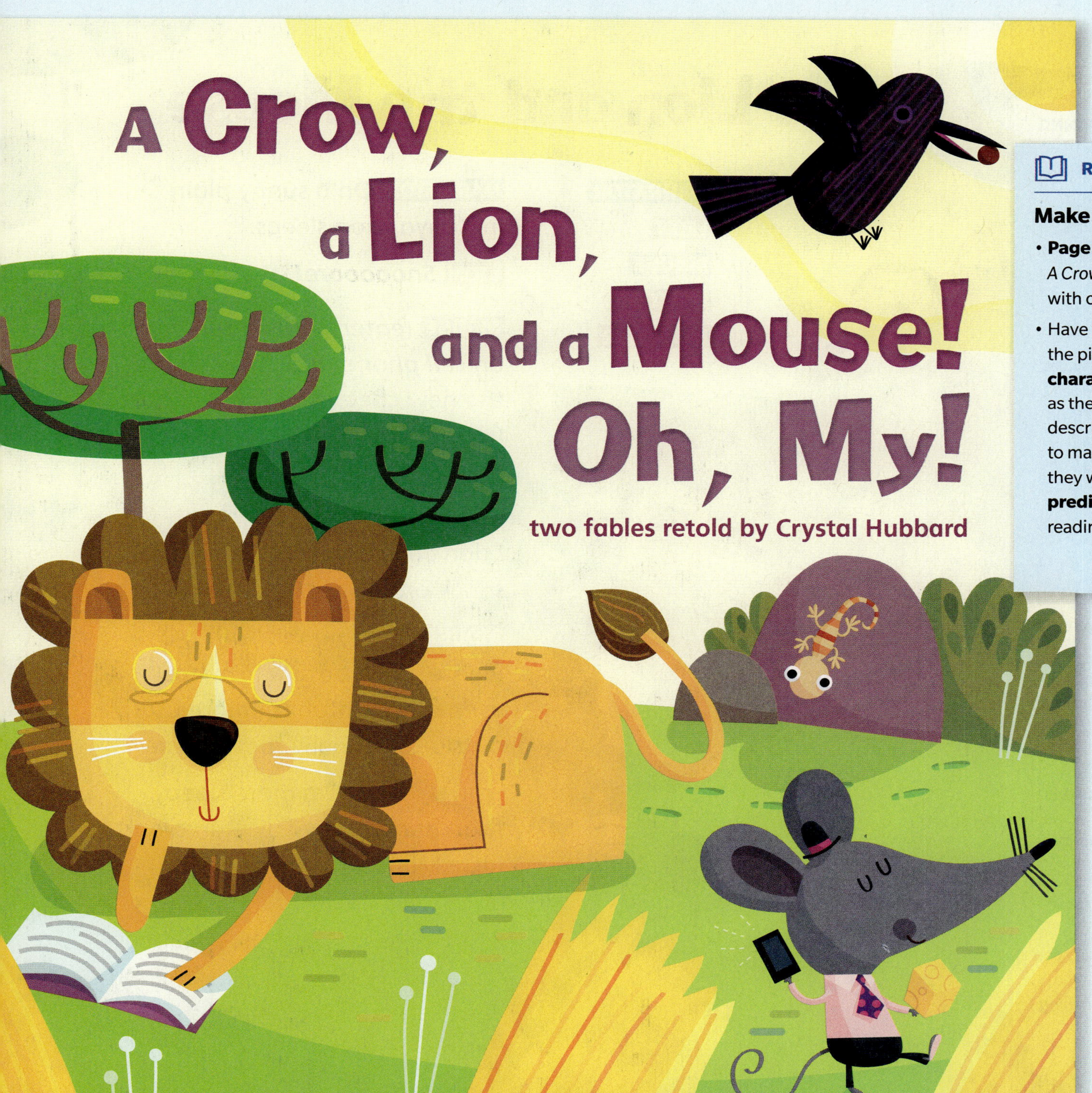

READ FOR UNDERSTANDING

Make Predictions

- **Page through** the beginning of *A Crow, a Lion, and a Mouse! Oh, My!* with children.
- Have them **use prior knowledge,** the pictures, as well as **characteristics of drama**, such as the cast of characters, setting description, and scene changes, to make predictions. Tell children they will **return to their predictions** after they finish reading.

DOK 2

READ FOR UNDERSTANDING

ASK: What is the setting? *(on a sunny plain in Kenya)* **Why is the setting important?** *(It helps the reader get a mental picture about where things are happening.)*

ANNOTATION TIP: Have children label the characters in the picture.

FOLLOW-UP: Why does Lion wake up? *(Mouse is talking loudly on a cell phone.)* **Why is Mouse fearful?** *(The illustration shows that Lion is much larger than Mouse; Mouse thinks Lion is going to eat him.)*

DOK 2

TARGETED CLOSE READ

Have children reread pages 154–155 to analyze elements of drama.

ANNOTATION TIP: Have children underline the stage directions.

ASK: What do the stage directions tell you? *(They give information about what the characters are doing and how they look and feel.)*

FOLLOW-UP: Why is the Narrator an important role? *(The Narrator gives information about the setting and what the characters are doing so the reader understands what is happening.)*

DOK 3

The Lion and the Mouse

CAST: NARRATOR, LION, MOUSE, HUNTER 1, HUNTER 2

NARRATOR On a sunny plain in Kenya, Lion sleeps.

LION ***Snooooore!***

MOUSE *(enters, noisily talking on cell phone)* Have you tasted the new cheeses at the Nairobi Food Mart? They're so good, and they're on sale!

LION *(wakes, grabs Mouse)* I don't like cheeses. I prefer to snack on ***meeses!*** I mean mice.

MOUSE *(looking fearful)* Please, don't eat me! I'm not even a mouthful. I'm more useful outside your belly than inside.

LION *(yawns)* I'm more sleepy than hungry anyway. Run along, little Mouse. *(falls asleep)*

154

NARRATOR Sleeping Lion cannot hear danger approach.

HUNTER 1 *(carrying a rope, whispers)* This lion will be our greatest prize!

HUNTER 2 *(helps Hunter 1 bind surprised Lion)* Let's get the truck!

NARRATOR Mighty Lion has a mighty big problem!

MOUSE *(nibbling cheese, drops cheese when he sees Lion)* Dude, what happened?

LION *(looking ashamed)* Hunters trapped me. I'm so embarrassed!

MOUSE Not for long!

NARRATOR Mouse's tiny, sharp teeth chewed and gnawed and tugged at the rope until it fell away.

LION I'm free! *(hugs Mouse)* I learned a lesson today. You're a better friend than a meal! *(Smiling, Lion and Mouse exit together.)*

155

READ FOR UNDERSTANDING

Create Mental Images

MODEL CREATING MENTAL IMAGES

THINK ALOUD *I read that after the hunters trap Lion by tying him up with rope, Mouse's "tiny sharp teeth chewed and gnawed and tugged at the rope." These words help me picture Mouse trying hard to free Lion. So I ask myself: I wonder if Lion will feel differently about Mouse if Mouse frees him. I'll read on.*

FOLLOW-UP: How do you picture Lion and Mouse exiting together? *(Possible response: They are walking side-by-side, holding hands, and smiling.)*

DOK 2

READ FOR UNDERSTANDING

Quick Teach Words

As needed to support children's comprehension, briefly explain the meaning of *exit* in this context.

- When characters in a play *exit*, they leave the scene. Actors playing the characters exit by leaving the stage.

TARGETED CLOSE READ

Elements of Drama

Have children reread page 156 to analyze elements of drama.

ASK: Find details in the dialogue that explain how Crow 1 and Crow 2 are different. *(Crow 1 is a problem solver. Crow 2 just likes to complain.)*

How can you tell the crows apart in the picture? *(The stage directions say that Crow 2's wings are crossed over his chest. So Crow 2 is blue.)*

ANNOTATION TIP: Have children label the crows in the picture.

FOLLOW-UP: How does the setting help you understand what is happening? *(The narrator says it is a hot summer day, so that helps me know why they want the water.)*

DOK 3

READ FOR UNDERSTANDING

Create Mental Images

ASK: What details help you imagine the weather? *("hottest day of summer")*

FOLLOW-UP: How do the details help you imagine how the crows feel? *(The crows are hot. Their mouths feel dry because they are very thirsty.)*

DOK 2

The Crow and the Pitcher

CAST: CROW 1
CROW 2
NARRATOR

NARRATOR On the hottest day of summer, two crows find a pitcher of water.

CROW 1 *(circling pitcher)* It's half full!

CROW 2 *(wings crossed over chest)* It's half empty.

CROW 1 *(tries to stick beak in pitcher)* The opening is too narrow!

CROW 2 *(tries to lift pitcher)* I can't hold it because I don't have thumbs!

156

NARRATOR The crows grow thirstier in the heat of the sizzling sun.

CROW 1 *(staring at pitcher)* There has to be a way to get that water.

CROW 2 *(kicking pebble on ground)* I wish I had ice cream. *(kicks a pebble)* Or an ice pop. *(kicks a pebble)*

CROW 1 I've got it! *(picks up a pebble)*

CROW 2 What are you doing with that?

CROW 1 *(drops pebble into pitcher)* You'll see.

157

Notice & Note

Again and Again

- **Remind children** that when an event happens over and over, they should stop to notice and note.
- **Have children** tell how they might use the strategy on page 157. *(Crow 2 kicks a pebble over and over.)*

ANNOTATION TIP: Have children circle the repetition in the text.

- **Remind them** of the Anchor Question: **Why might the author bring this up again and again?** *(Seeing Crow 2 kick the pebble over and over makes Crow 1 think of a way to solve their problem.)*

DOK 3

READ FOR UNDERSTANDING

Phonics/Decoding in Context

Have children point to the word *way*. Review how the vowel team *ay* makes the long *a* sound. **Model blending** the sounds and saying the word. Have children repeat.

CROW 2 Are you making Pebble-ade?

CROW 1 *(picks up pebble, drops it in pitcher)* Just keep watching and you'll see how smart I am!

READ FOR UNDERSTANDING

Create Mental Images

MODEL CREATING MENTAL IMAGES

THINK ALOUD *I read that Crow 2 thinks Crow 1 is "doing great." I think Crow 2 is saying that so he won't have to help. I imagine Crow 2 relaxing on a tree branch and watching Crow 1 work. He's smiling as he tells Crow 1 how great he's doing. I can imagine Crow 1 is looking up at him and rolling his eyes as he gathers more pebbles.)*

DOK 2

NARRATOR This clever crow can't get to the water, so he's making the water get to him.

CROW 2 *(impressed)* Wow! The water is rising!

CROW 1 *(spits out pebble)* It would rise faster if both of us put in pebbles. *(picks up pebble)*

CROW 2 No, that's okay. You're doing great.

CROW 1 *(drops pebble in pitcher)* There! I can finally get a drink. *(begins sipping water)*

CROW 2 *(behind Crow 1)* Hurry, I want a turn! Save some for me!

READ FOR UNDERSTANDING

Wrap Up

Revisit the predictions children made before reading. Have them confirm or correct their predictions using evidence from the text and illustrations.

DOK 2

Respond to Reading

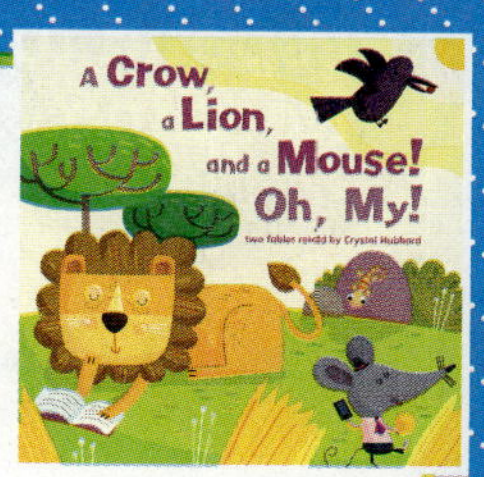

Use details from *A Crow, a Lion, and a Mouse! Oh, My!* to answer these questions with a partner.

1. **Create Mental Images** When Mouse sees what happened to Lion, he is so surprised he drops his cheese. What does Mouse see? Use details in the text to help you picture it in your mind. Then describe your picture to a partner.

2. How is the narrator's part different from the other parts in each drama?

3. Why is a fable a good way to teach a lesson? What lessons do you learn from these two fables?

Listening Tip

Look at your partner as you listen. Nod your head to show you are interested.

159

Academic Discussion

Use the **TURN AND TALK** routine. Remind children to follow agreed-upon rules for discussion, such as looking at their partner as they listen and nodding to show they're paying attention.

Possible responses:

1. *Lion is tied up by ropes so tight that he can't move. He looks embarrassed when he sees that Mouse is there.* DOK 2
2. *The narrator doesn't talk to the other characters. The narrator describes the action and helps to explain the setting.* DOK 3
3. *A fable is a good way to teach a lesson because fables are fun to read. The lesson I learned from "The Lion and the Mouse" is to be kind. The lesson I learned from "The Crow and the Pitcher" is not to give up.* DOK 3

Respond to Reading

Write a Thank-You Note

PROMPT How do you think Lion feels about what Mouse did to help him? Use details from the words and pictures to explain your ideas.

PLAN First, add words to the web that describe how you think Lion feels after Mouse helps him.

160

Write About Reading

- **Read aloud** the prompt.
- **Lead a discussion** in which children share their ideas about what Mouse did to help Lion and how Lion feels as a result. Tell them to use text evidence to support their ideas.
- Then read aloud the Plan section. Have children use ideas from the discussion in their web.

DOK 3

WRITE Now write a note from Lion to Mouse thanking him for his help. Remember to:

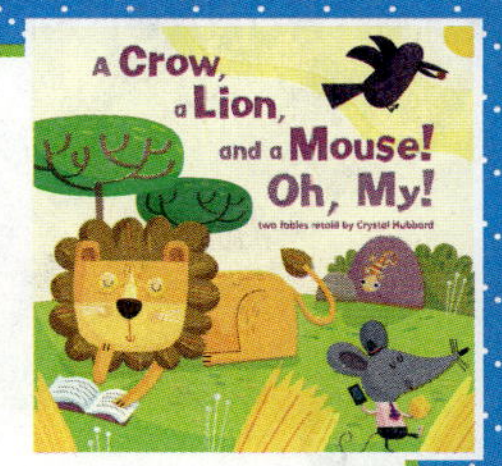

- Include details from the drama that explain why Lion is thanking Mouse.
- Begin your note with *Dear Mouse*. End it with *Your friend, Lion*.

Responses will vary.

Write About Reading

- **Read aloud** the Write section.
- **Encourage children** to include details from the play that explain what Mouse did and why Lion is thanking him.
- **Remind children** that a note to someone begins with a greeting to the person receiving the note and ends with a signature from the sender.

DOK 3

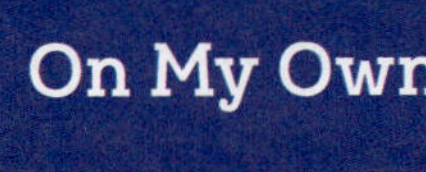

Independent Close Read

Have children close read and annotate "The Wind and the Sun" on their own during small-group or independent work time. As needed, **use the Scaffolded Support notes** that follow to guide children who need additional help.

Scaffolded Support

As needed, remind children to:

- look for descriptive language in the story that helps them create mental images as they read.
- use details in the text and pictures to identify elements of drama: the cast of characters, dialogue, information about the setting, and stage directions.

DOK 3

Prepare to Read

GENRE STUDY **Dramas** are plays that are read and performed.

MAKE A PREDICTION Preview "The Wind and the Sun." Wind and Sun disagree. You know that dramas have characters, dialogue, and a setting. What do you think this drama will be about?

The Sun and Wind might be having an argument about who is better.

SET A PURPOSE Read to find out how Wind and Sun decide to settle their disagreement.

162

The Wind and the Sun

READ Circle words that create a picture in your mind.

Cast of Characters: Bob, Narrator, Sun, Wind
Setting: a cool spring day in the country

NARRATOR: Up in the sky, a disagreement is beginning.

WIND: I don't mean to brag, but I am the very most powerful force in the universe.

SUN: I disagree, my friend. My power is greater.

WIND: No way! Think about it. I can twist myself into a giant tornado if I want to.

SUN: Yes, but my warmth and light can make tiny seeds grow into mighty trees.

WIND: Let's settle this once and for all.

NARRATOR: Just then, they saw a man taking a walk. He was wearing a warm, woolly coat.

Close Reading Tip

Underline words that tell about the setting.

Scaffolded Support

As needed, remind children that:

- identifying and thinking about words that appeal to the senses—sight, sound, taste, smell, and touch—can help readers create mental pictures.
- the setting, or time and place, is often identified at the beginning of a drama.

DOK 2

READ How do stage directions tell more about the characters?

SUN: How about this? Whoever can get Bob to take his coat off is the winner.

WIND: Oh boy, this is going to be so easy. *(blowing) Whoosh!*

NARRATOR: Bob shivers a little bit.

WIND: *(blowing harder) Whoosh! Whooosh! Whoooooosh!*

BOB: My, it sure is windy. I better button up. *Brrrr!*

SUN: Let me give it a try. I will turn up my heat and SHINE!

NARRATOR: Bob smiles and takes off his coat.

BOB: Wow, that sun feels great. What a funny day.

WIND: Sunny, you won this fair and square. I think I've learned a lesson, my friend.

SUN: *(smiling)* Being gentle is a very great power.

Close Reading Tip

Underline the lesson that Wind learns.

Scaffolded Support

As needed, remind children that:

- noticing how the setting causes events or actions to happen can help them understand why it is important.
- looking for ways that a character changes from the beginning of a drama to the end can help them identify the lesson the character learns.

DOK 3

CHECK MY UNDERSTANDING

How is the setting an important part of this drama?

The setting is important because the man had to be outside for Sun and Wind to make him take his coat off.

Cite Text Evidence

WRITE ABOUT IT How would Bob tell the story? Write the events in order the way Bob would tell them. Describe what Bob was thinking, feeling, and doing on his walk.

First, I went out for a walk. It was cool, so I wore my coat. Next, it got very windy. I felt cold, so I buttoned up. Last, it got warm, so I took off my coat.

Scaffolded Support

As needed, guide children to use details from the drama and their knowledge of Bob's character to determine how he might describe the events. **Remind children** to use words like *first, next,* and *last* to indicate the order of the events.

DOK 3

READ FOR UNDERSTANDING

Introduce the Text

- **Read aloud** and discuss the information about the genre.
- Guide children to **set a purpose** for reading to practice making and confirming predictions.
- **Provide information** about the background topic, Hollywood.
- **Tell children** to look for and think about the Power Words as they read.

Guided Practice

Prepare to Read

GENRE STUDY **Fantasies** are stories with events that could not really happen. As you read *Hollywood Chicken,* look for:

- animal characters that talk and act like real people
- the beginning, middle, and ending of the story
- problems and solutions

SET A PURPOSE You know that most stories include a problem. Use what you know about the text to make a **prediction,** or good guess, about the problem in this story. Read to see if you are right. If not, make a new prediction.

POWER WORDS

- journey
- fulfill
- believe
- speech

Build Background: Hollywood

166

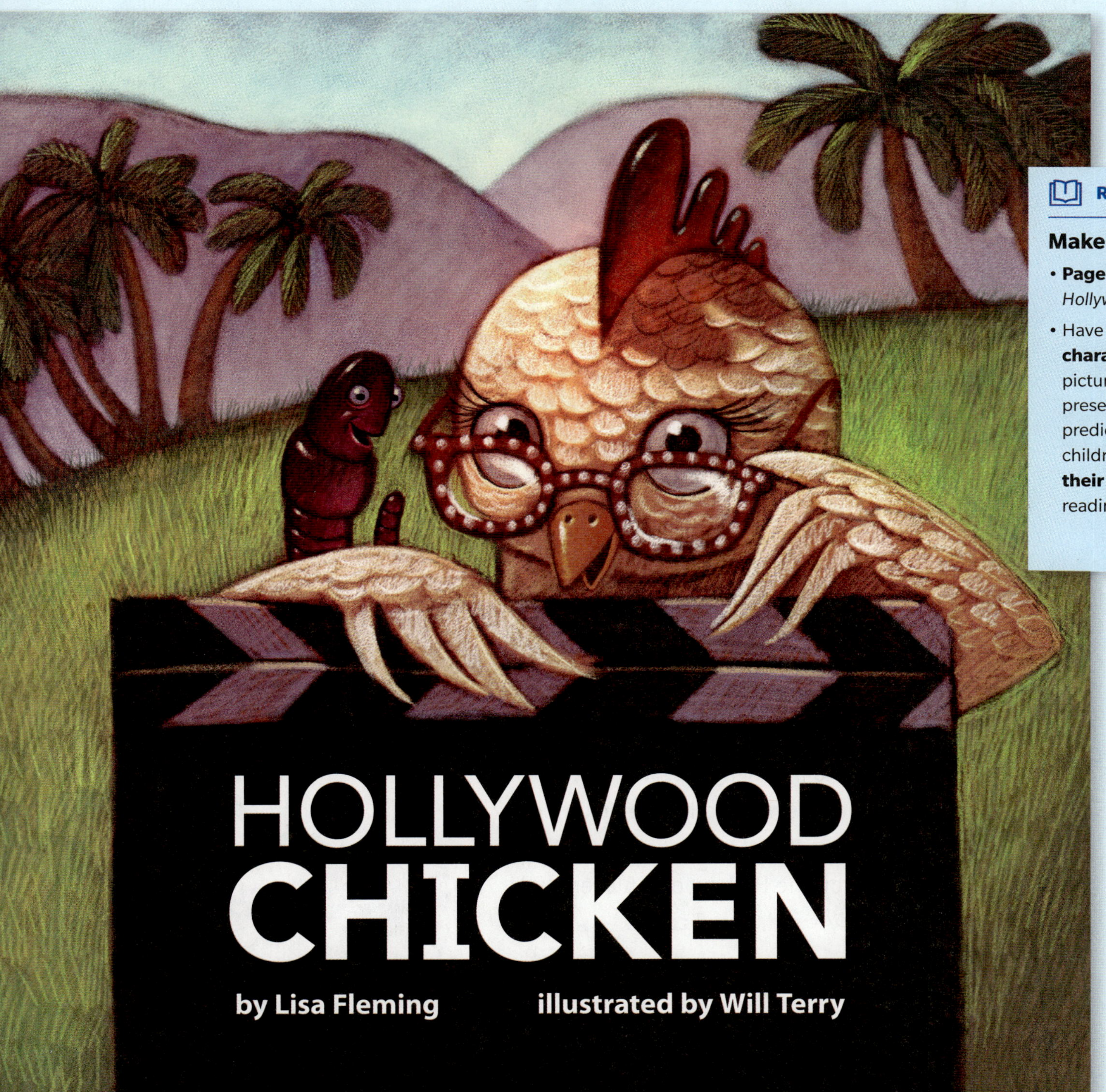

READ FOR UNDERSTANDING

Make Predictions

- **Page through** the beginning of *Hollywood Chicken* with children.
- Have them **use prior knowledge, characteristics of the genre,** the pictures, and the way the story is presented as a series of messages to predict what it will be about. Tell children that they will **return to their predictions** after they finish reading the story.

DOK 2

READ FOR UNDERSTANDING

ASK: Whose words are on this page? What is this character writing? *(They are Chicken Lily's words. She is writing a letter.)*

FOLLOW-UP: How do the words and picture help you understand this? *(The words look like a letter on the page. The letter is addressed to "Ms. Luz Cruz." It is signed, "Sincerely, Chicken Lily." The picture shows Chicken Lily typing on her computer. There is an arrow pointing from the computer to the letter, so I know that's what she is typing.)*

DOK 3

READ FOR UNDERSTANDING

ASK: What problem does Chicken Lily have? *(She does not like her quiet life on the farm. She wants to go to Hollywood and become a famous actress.)*

DOK 2

Dear Ms. Luz Cruz,

I can't wait to fly this coop! Life in these green hills is dull, dull, dull. The endless farmland, quiet evenings, and the steady diet of corn and more corn just aren't enough for me. I need more from life! How I dream of being on stage! I want to make my way in the city where dreams come true! I could be the next poultry actress to make it big! I, Chicken Lily, will have my own star on the Hollywood Chicken Walk of Fame! Hollywood, here I come!

Sincerely,
Chicken Lily

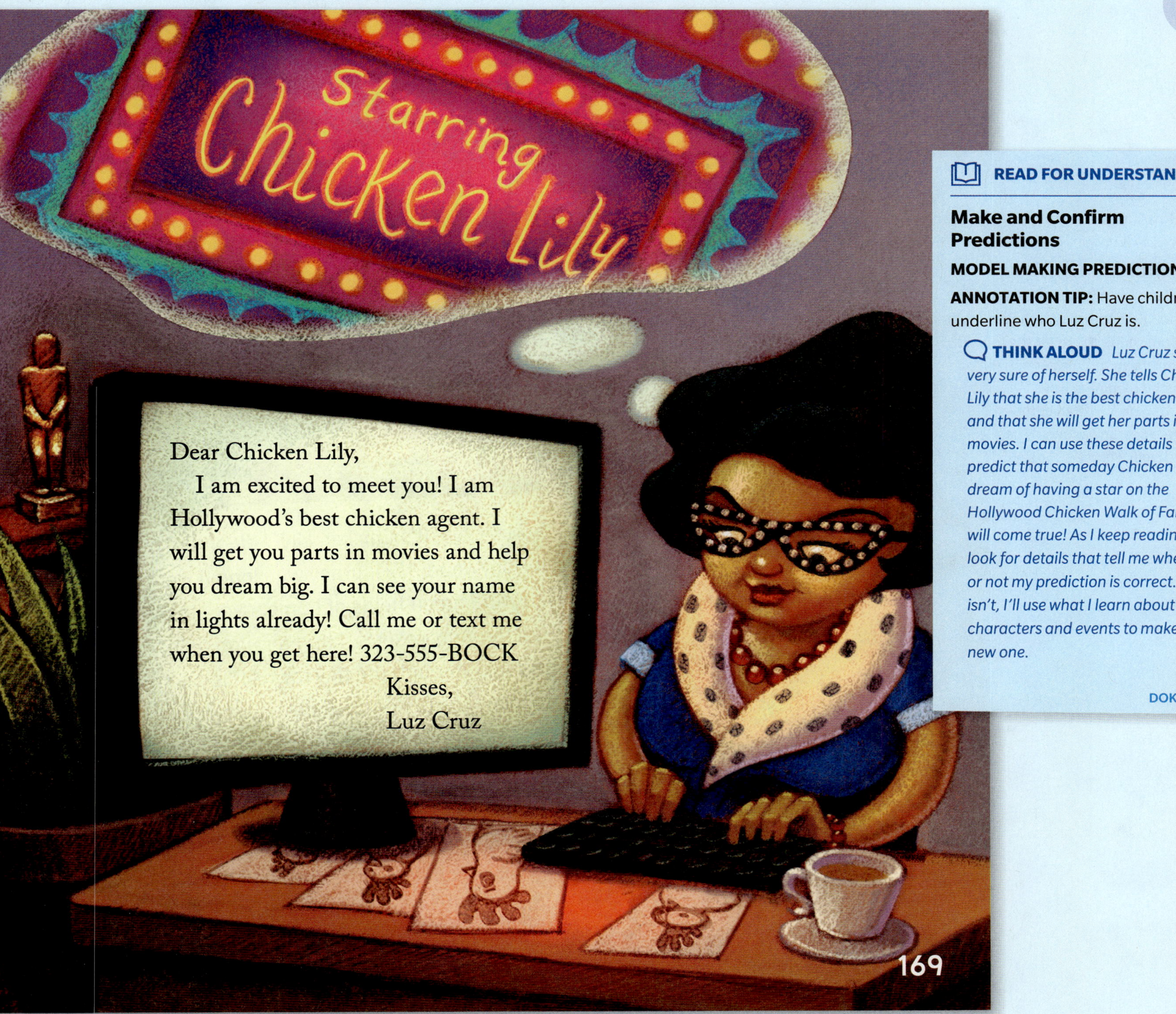

Dear Chicken Lily,

I am excited to meet you! I am Hollywood's best chicken agent. I will get you parts in movies and help you dream big. I can see your name in lights already! Call me or text me when you get here! 323-555-BOCK

Kisses,

Luz Cruz

169

READ FOR UNDERSTANDING

Make and Confirm Predictions

MODEL MAKING PREDICTIONS

ANNOTATION TIP: Have children underline who Luz Cruz is.

THINK ALOUD *Luz Cruz sounds very sure of herself. She tells Chicken Lily that she is the best chicken agent and that she will get her parts in movies. I can use these details to predict that someday Chicken Lily's dream of having a star on the Hollywood Chicken Walk of Fame will come true! As I keep reading, I will look for details that tell me whether or not my prediction is correct. If it isn't, I'll use what I learn about the characters and events to make a new one.*

DOK 2

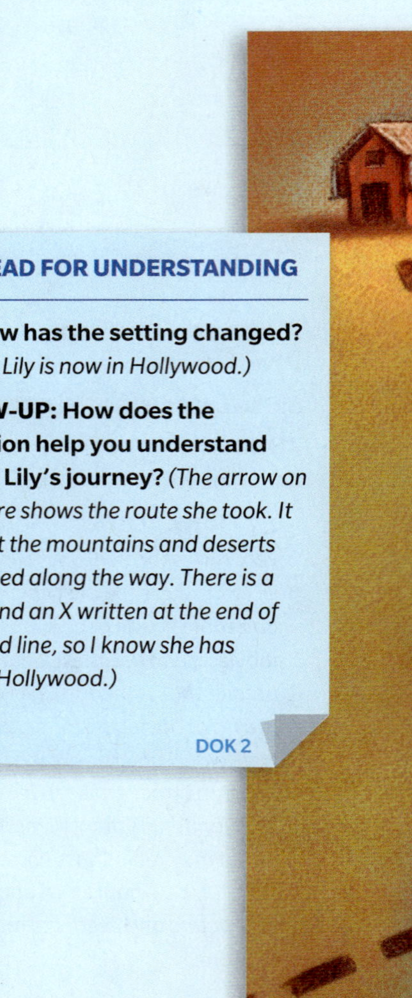

READ FOR UNDERSTANDING

ASK: How has the setting changed? *(Chicken Lily is now in Hollywood.)*

FOLLOW-UP: How does the illustration help you understand Chicken Lily's journey? *(The arrow on the picture shows the route she took. It goes past the mountains and deserts she crossed along the way. There is a big city and an X written at the end of the dotted line, so I know she has reached Hollywood.)*

DOK 2

Ms. Cruz, it's Chicken Lily. I did it! I'm here in Hollywood! My journey was long. I went from the wide green fields of home, over mountains, and through deserts. I had a rough time crossing through the tiny towns filled with homes and cars and people. There was a close call with a cat in Burbank, but I made it!

Oh, the city! It's everything I dreamed it would be! It's big, busy, and beautiful! The buildings are so tall. There are so many people. The noise of the city is so different than the quiet of my home on the farm.

170

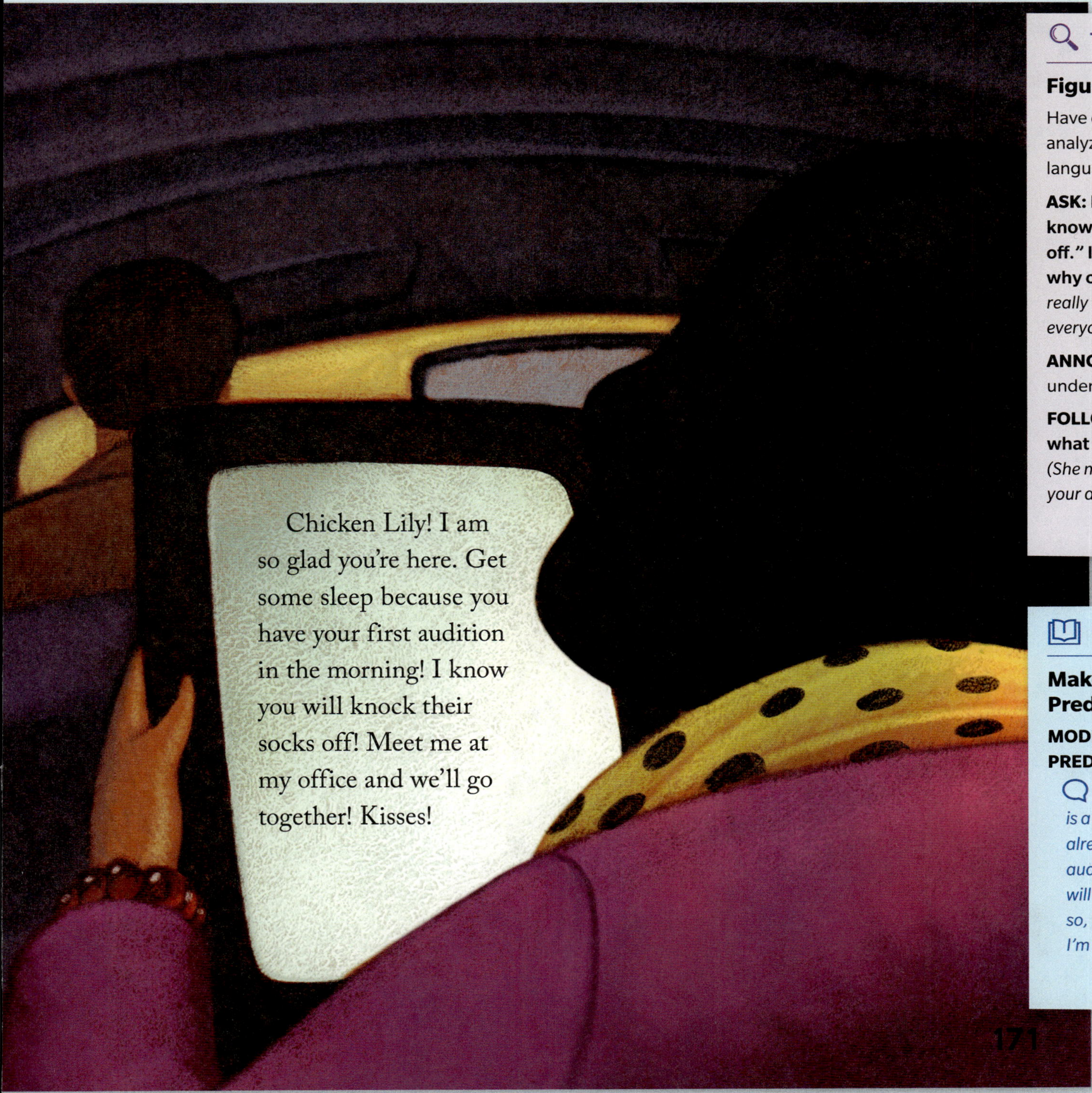

Chicken Lily! I am so glad you're here. Get some sleep because you have your first audition in the morning! I know you will knock their socks off! Meet me at my office and we'll go together! Kisses!

171

TARGETED CLOSE READ

Figurative Language

Have children reread page 171 to analyze the use of figurative language.

ASK: Luz tells Chicken Lily that she knows "you will knock their socks off." Is this literal language? Explain why or why not. *(No. Luz does not really think that Lily will take off everyone's socks.)*

ANNOTATION TIP: Have children underline the idiom.

FOLLOW-UP: How might Luz say what she means in a literal way? *(She might say, "I know they will love your acting.")*

DOK 3

READ FOR UNDERSTANDING

Make and Confirm Predictions

MODEL CONFIRMING PREDICTIONS

 **THINK ALOUD:** *Wow! Luz Cruz is a good chicken agent. She has already gotten Chicken Lily an audition. She believes Chicken Lily will do well and get the part. I think so, too. I will read on to see if I'm right.*

DOK 2

TARGETED CLOSE READ

Figurative Language

Have children reread pages 172–173 to analyze the use of figurative language.

ANNOTATION TIP: Have children underline the similes on pages 172–173 and circle the word *as* in each simile.

ASK: On page 172, what does Chicken Lily compare herself to when answering Luz? *(a peacock)*

FOLLOW-UP: Why does she do this? *(A peacock looks very proud when it opens all the feathers of its tail. Comparing herself to a peacock shows how proud Lily is that she got the part.)*

FOLLOW-UP: What details in the text explain what the simile on page 173 means? *(In her diary, Lily compares herself to a little chick who can't help itself. She decides not to let Luz Cruz know there's a problem on the set because she doesn't want her to think she can't do anything on her own.)*

DOK 3

Dear Chicken Diary,

Today I got to meet the other actors on my movie. So many of them have gone to big chicken acting schools. A lot have come from families where the chickens all work in the movies. What if I don't fit in?

One of the actors sure made me feel like I don't belong. Slim the Worm made a joke about the way I talk. He didn't think I heard him, but I did.

Did I make the wrong decision when I left the farm? What if I can't fulfill my dream? Maybe I should let Luz Cruz know there is a problem on the set. I don't want her to think I'm as helpless as a chick, though.

173

READ FOR UNDERSTANDING

ASK: How is this message different from the ones you have read so far? *(Chicken Lily is not writing this message to Luz Cruz. It is an entry in her diary.)*

FOLLOW-UP: How does this help you learn more about Chicken Lily? *(She is able to share feelings and worries in her diary that she might not want to tell Luz Cruz. She can be more honest because she knows no one else will read it.)*

DOK 3

READ FOR UNDERSTANDING

Make and Confirm Predictions

ASK: Why does Chicken Lily feel that she may not fit in? *(Some actors have gone to big chicken acting schools. Slim the Worm made a joke about the way she talks.)*

FOLLOW-UP: Use what you learn in Chicken Lily's diary entry to make a new prediction. *(Possible response: I don't think Lily will tell Cruz there is a problem on the set. She will try her best and do a good job acting.)*

DOK 2

READ FOR UNDERSTANDING

ASK: How much time has passed since the last diary entry? *(six months)*

ANNOTATION TIP: Have children circle the text that indicates this.

FOLLOW-UP: What has happened to Lily's acting career in that time? Respond with evidence from the words and pictures. *(Lily has become a successful actress. Her first movie was a hit. She is about to make another movie. In the picture, she looks very sure of herself and her acting skills.)*

ASK: Why are the titles of the movies funny? *(The titles all have to do with the riddle* Why Did the Chicken Cross the Road?*)*

DOK 2

 **READ FOR UNDERSTANDING**

Phonics/Decoding in Context

Have children point to the word *Highway*. Review how the vowel team *ay* can stand for the long *a* sound anywhere in a word. **Guide them to blend** the letters in each syllable and say the word.

Six months later . . .

Dear Chicken Diary,

Who would believe it? *Crossing the Road: The Other Side* is a smash hit! The movie's success has made me want to work even harder. I started taking a chicken acting class. Every day I meet with my friends to practice my acting skills. I think it is paying off. We start filming *Crossing the Road 2: The Highway* tomorrow!

174

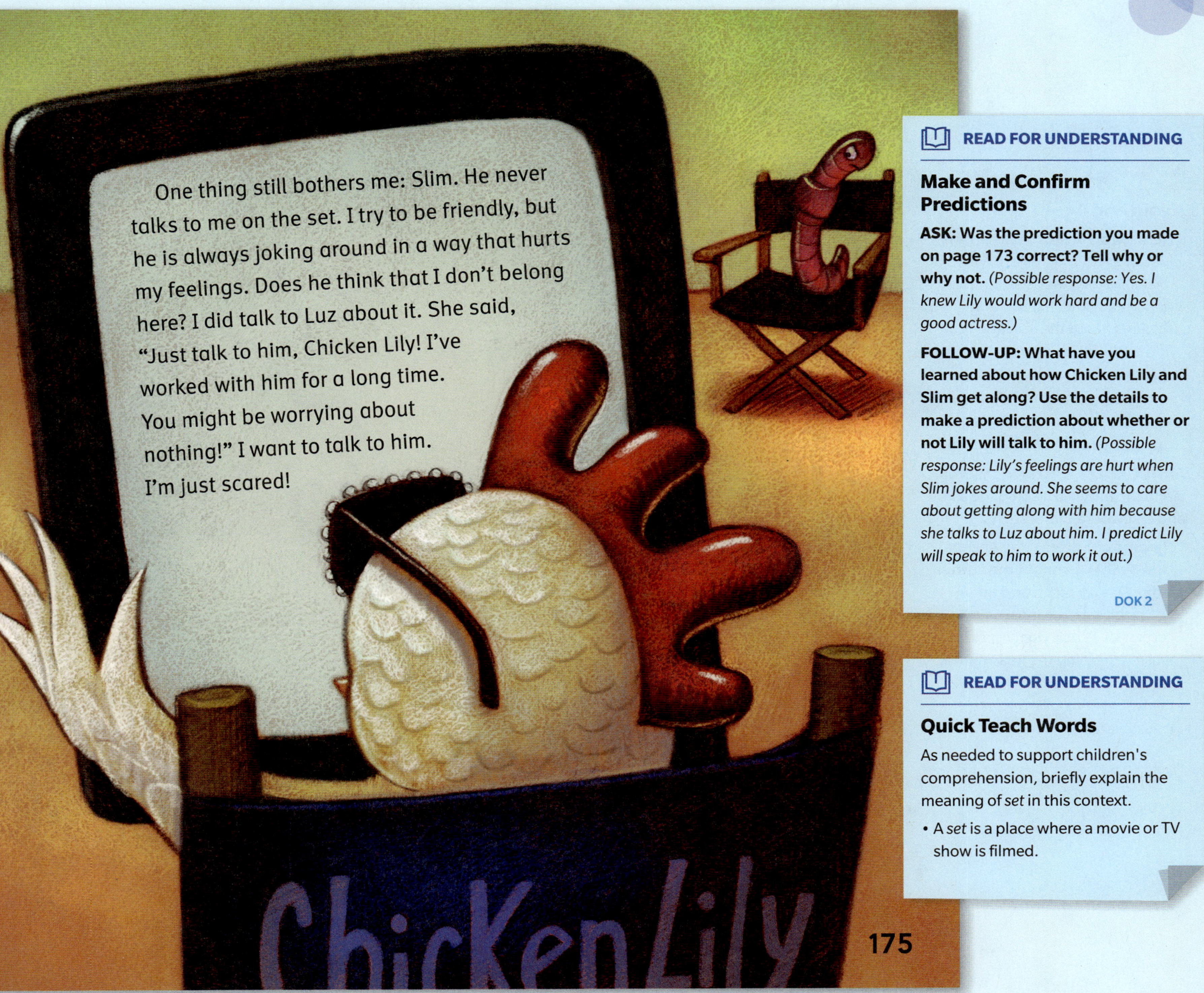

One thing still bothers me: Slim. He never talks to me on the set. I try to be friendly, but he is always joking around in a way that hurts my feelings. Does he think that I don't belong here? I did talk to Luz about it. She said, "Just talk to him, Chicken Lily! I've worked with him for a long time. You might be worrying about nothing!" I want to talk to him. I'm just scared!

175

READ FOR UNDERSTANDING

Make and Confirm Predictions

ASK: Was the prediction you made on page 173 correct? Tell why or why not. *(Possible response: Yes. I knew Lily would work hard and be a good actress.)*

FOLLOW-UP: What have you learned about how Chicken Lily and Slim get along? Use the details to make a prediction about whether or not Lily will talk to him. *(Possible response: Lily's feelings are hurt when Slim jokes around. She seems to care about getting along with him because she talks to Luz about him. I predict Lily will speak to him to work it out.)*

DOK 2

READ FOR UNDERSTANDING

Quick Teach Words

As needed to support children's comprehension, briefly explain the meaning of *set* in this context.

- A *set* is a place where a movie or TV show is filmed.

Notice & Note

Again and Again

- **Remind children** that when an idea or event is repeated over and over in a story, they should stop to notice and note. Explain that thinking about the repetition can inform their predictions.
- **Have children** explain why they might use this strategy on page 176. *(Chicken Lily keeps making* Crossing the Road *movies.)*

ANNOTATION TIP: Have children circle the movie title on page 176 and elsewhere in the story.

- **Remind children** of the Anchor Question: **Why might the author bring this up again and again?** *(It shows that Lily has become successful. People want her to keep making* Crossing the Road *movies. Also, the names of the movies are funny. They make the story more enjoyable to read.)*

DOK 3

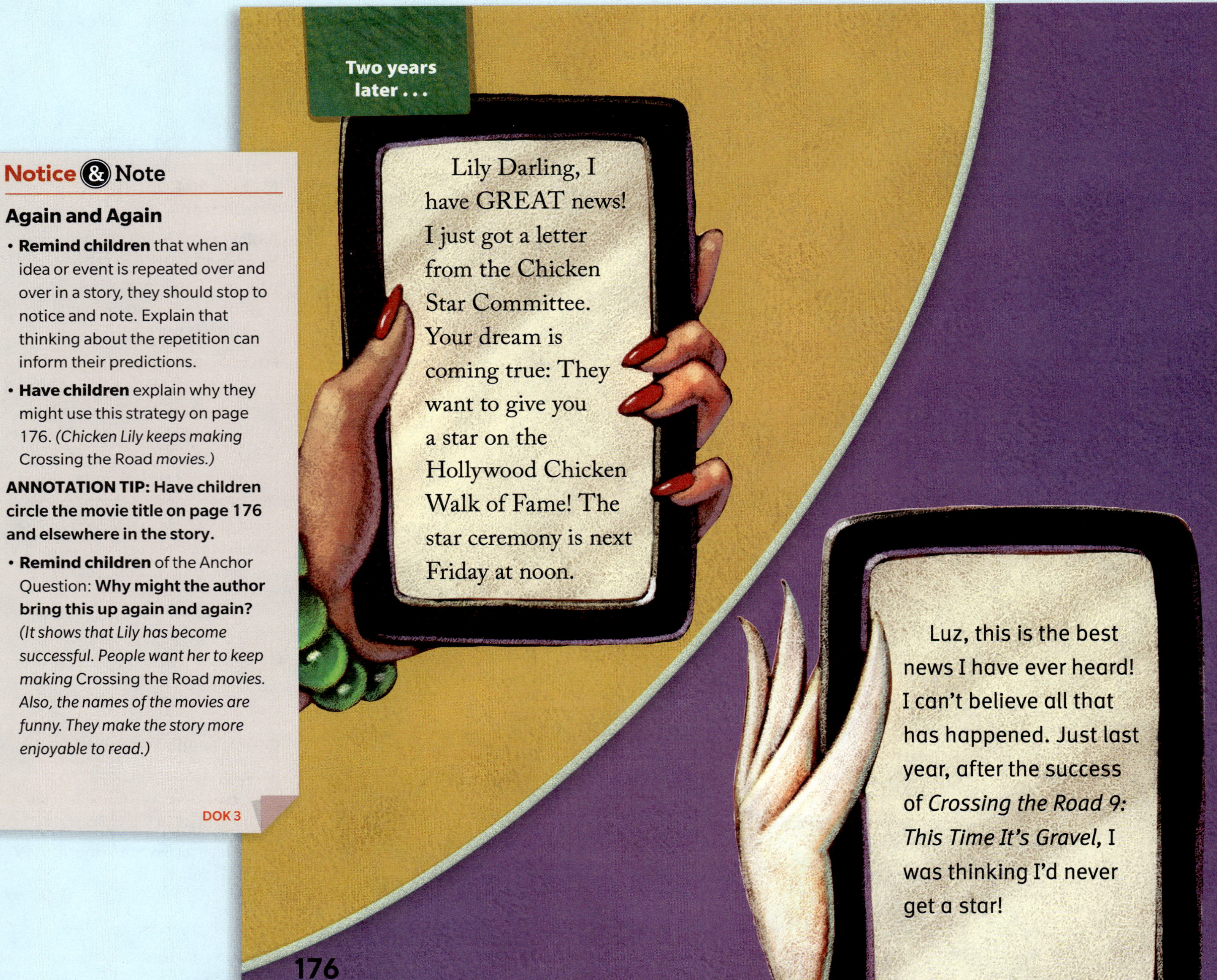

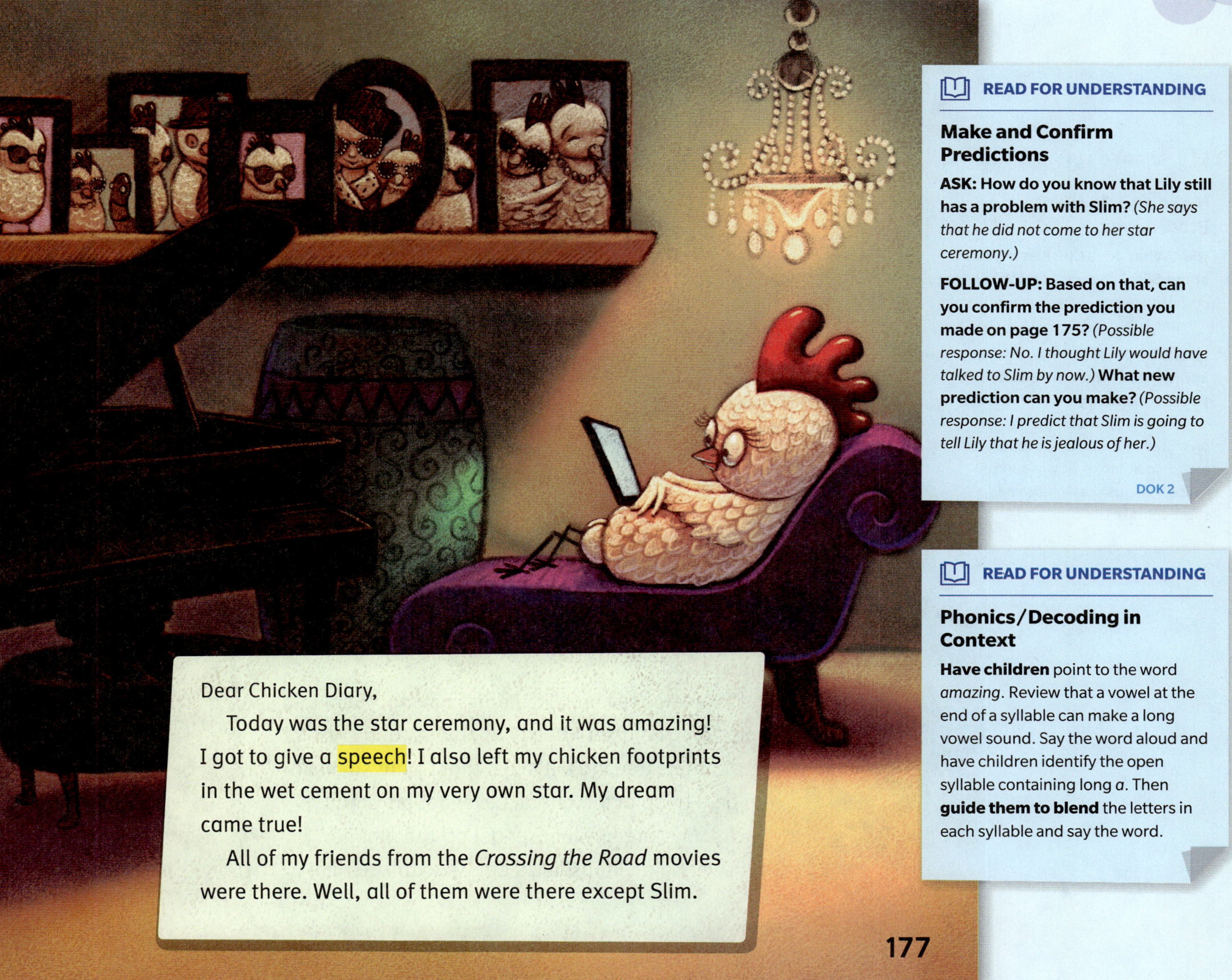

READ FOR UNDERSTANDING

Make and Confirm Predictions

ASK: How do you know that Lily still has a problem with Slim? *(She says that he did not come to her star ceremony.)*

FOLLOW-UP: Based on that, can you confirm the prediction you made on page 175? *(Possible response: No. I thought Lily would have talked to Slim by now.)* **What new prediction can you make?** *(Possible response: I predict that Slim is going to tell Lily that he is jealous of her.)*

DOK 2

READ FOR UNDERSTANDING

Phonics/Decoding in Context

Have children point to the word *amazing*. Review that a vowel at the end of a syllable can make a long vowel sound. Say the word aloud and have children identify the open syllable containing long *a*. Then **guide them to blend** the letters in each syllable and say the word.

 READ FOR UNDERSTANDING

Make and Confirm Predictions

ASK: What does Chicken Lily learn about Slim? *(He wasn't mean to her on purpose. He was joking because he felt nervous.)*

FOLLOW-UP: How does this information affect the prediction you made on page 177? *(Possible answer: It confirms my prediction. I predicted that Slim would tell Lily he was jealous. I think he was sort of jealous because he wants to be successful like Lily.)*

DOK 2

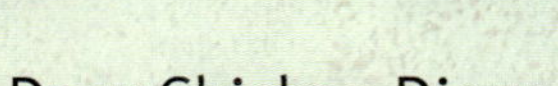

Dear Chicken Diary,

On my way home, I saw Slim sitting alone on a park bench. I took a chance and asked him what was wrong. He seemed so surprised that I had asked.

"Sometimes I feel like I don't belong," Slim told me. "I make jokes when I'm nervous, and I know I hurt others' feelings. It's just that I want so much to be a good actor, but all I ever get are small parts. My career will never get off the ground." I was very glad I took Luz's advice to talk to him!

178

READ FOR UNDERSTANDING

Make and Confirm Predictions

ASK: How does Slim remind you of Chicken Lily? Use details from the story to explain. *(Like Slim, Chicken Lily sometimes feels like she doesn't belong. When she first started acting, she was worried that she might not fit in with the other chicken actors.)*

FOLLOW-UP: What do you predict Chicken Lily will say to Slim? *(Possible answer: Chicken Lily will give Slim advice, just like Luz gave advice to her. I think she will tell him that things will get better for him.)*

DOK 2

I put my arm around Slim and told him my story. I told him about my journey from the farm and how I had wondered if I would ever fit in. I told him about my years and years of practice and hard work. And I told him that I would help him make his dreams come true. Maybe some day, my friend Slim might be the first worm to have a star on the Hollywood Chicken Walk of Fame.

180

READ FOR UNDERSTANDING

Make and Confirm Predictions

ASK: How does the story end? *(Chicken Lily gives Slim advice about making his dreams come true. They become friends.)*

FOLLOW-UP: Does the ending confirm the prediction you made on page 179? Tell why or why not. *(Possible answer: The ending confirms my prediction. Chicken Lily helps Slim by telling him about her own experience.)*

DOK 2

READ FOR UNDERSTANDING

Wrap-Up

Revisit the predictions children made before reading. Have them confirm or correct their predictions using evidence from the text and illustrations.

DOK 2

Respond to Reading

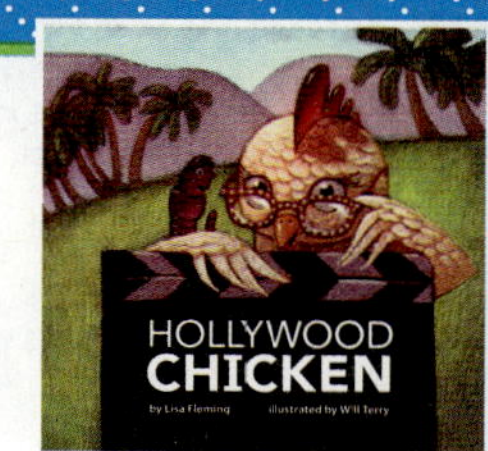

Use details from *Hollywood Chicken* to answer these questions with a partner.

1. **Make and Confirm Predictions** What predictions did you make about the problem and resolution before and as you read? What were you right about? What was different?

2. How do the places where Lily lives change in the story? What clues do you see in the pictures about her success?

3. How does Lily feel when she talks to Slim at the end of the story? How does she show her feelings?

Listening Tip

Listen carefully and politely. Look at your partner to show you are paying attention.

Academic Discussion

Use the TURN AND TALK routine. Remind children to follow agreed-upon rules for discussion, such as listening carefully and politely and looking at their partner to show they are paying attention.

Possible responses:

1. *Answers will vary.* DOK 2
2. *Chicken Lily starts out in the country on a farm. Then she moves to Hollywood. First, she is in a small room with a little bit of furniture. Later, she is in a big room with fancy furniture and lots of pictures of her as a movie star. This tells me that she is doing well in Hollywood.* DOK 2
3. *Lily feels glad that she took Luz's advice to talk to him. She shows Slim that she cares about his feelings by putting her arm around him and explaining that she used to feel like she didn't fit in, too.* DOK 3

Respond to Reading

Write a Movie Ad

PROMPT Movie ads use words and pictures to get people excited about seeing a movie. What would a movie ad for *Crossing the Road: The Other Side* be like? Look for details in the words and pictures to help you think of ideas.

PLAN First, think of an exciting scene that might be in the movie. Draw it. Add the title and the names of the stars.

Write About Reading

- **Read aloud** the prompt.
- **Lead a discussion** in which children share their ideas about what a movie ad for *Crossing the Road: The Other Side* would be like. Tell them to use text evidence from the story to support their ideas.
- Then read aloud the Plan section. Have children use ideas from their discussion to draw a scene that might be in the movie. Remind them that an ad with a scene that looks fun and exciting is more likely to get people to see the movie.

DOK 3

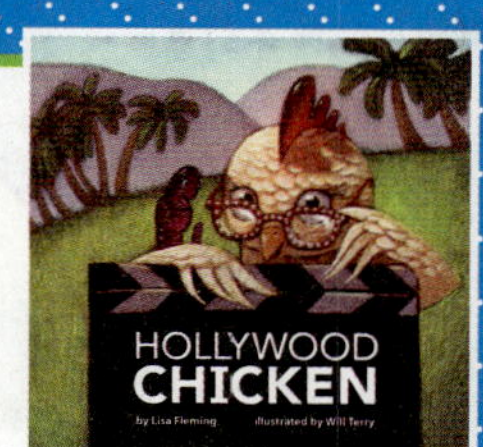

WRITE Now ask yourself what would make you want to see this movie. Write sentences that would persuade other kids to want to see it, too. Remember to:

- Include details about the movie's stars and setting.
- Use describing words such as *greatest*, *silliest*, and *stupendous*.

Responses will vary.

183

Write About Reading

- **Read aloud** the Write section.
- **Encourage children** to include describing words that help people picture the movie's characters, setting, and events and what is exciting about them.

DOK 3

Independent Close Read

Have children close read and annotate "The Best View" on their own during small-group or independent work time. As needed, **use the Scaffolded Support notes** that follow to guide children who need additional help.

Scaffolded Support

As needed, remind children to:

- use text features, pictures, and what they know about the genre to make a prediction before they begin reading the story. They can continue to make and confirm predictions as they read.
- look for the author's use of figurative language, or words and phrases that have a meaning different from their literal meaning.

DOK 2

Prepare to Read

GENRE STUDY **Fantasies** are stories with made-up events that could not really happen.

MAKE A PREDICTION Preview "The Best View." Two friends disagree about where to view a sunset. You know that a fantasy has make-believe events. What do you think will happen in this story?

I think that one friend will become angry with the other friend because they disagree about the best place to view the sunset.

SET A PURPOSE Read to understand a lesson learned by one of the characters and to see if your prediction is right. If not, think about what a fantasy story is like and make a new prediction.

The Best View

READ Underline two similes. How do they make the story interesting to read?

One summer evening, Hal and Joy decided to watch the sunset. They climbed a tall tree. It was a lovely, peaceful spot.

"The view is like a dream," Joy sighed. "It reminds me of my favorite poem. It goes…"

CLICK! Hal took a picture with his phone. He looked at the screen and frowned. "I don't think this is the best view," he said. "Let's try a taller tree."

"OK, but we have to run like the wind," Joy said. "It's almost sunset time."

She and Hal climbed an even taller tree with an even prettier view.

Scaffolded Support

As needed remind children that:

- similes use the word *like* or *as* to compare two things that might not seem alike at first.
- characters often give their opinions by saying words like "I think" or "I believe." A character can also state an opinion with describing words that tell how he or she feels about something.

DOK 2

Close Reading Tip

Mark the characters' opinions with a *.

READ What words help you picture the sunset? Underline them.

"Look how that fiery orange sun reflects on the shimmery water," Joy began. "It looks like…"

CLICK! Hal took another photo, looked at his screen, and frowned again. "Can you believe it? That bird just photobombed my sunset."

"Put that away," Joy groaned. "You are missing a stunning sunset!" But it was too late. The sun went down. Hal felt blue.

"Don't worry," Joy said. "We can come back tomorrow and watch the sunrise."

The next morning, Hal left his phone at home. He and Joy watched a beautiful sunrise together. It was as pretty as a picture.

Close Reading Tip

Put a ! by a surprising part.

Scaffolded Support

As needed, remind children that:

- authors often use sense words to help the reader imagine what is happening in the text.
- as they read, they should stop every so often to decide whether or not they can confirm a prediction they made earlier. If not, they can change their predictions or make new ones as they continue to read.

DOK 3

CHECK MY UNDERSTANDING

Think about the predictions you made before and during reading. Were they correct? Tell why or why not.

Responses will vary.

Cite Text Evidence

WRITE ABOUT IT What lesson does Hal learn? Use details from the text to explain your answer.

Hal learns that if he pays too much attention to his phone, he might miss important things going on around him.

187

Scaffolded Support

As needed, guide children to identify the lesson Hal learns by looking for details that tell how he changes and then thinking about what caused the change.

DOK 2

READ FOR UNDERSTANDING

Introduce the Text

- **Read aloud** and discuss the information about the genre.
- **Guide children** to set a purpose for reading to practice making connections.
- **Provide information** about the author, Pleasant DeSpain.
- **Tell children** to look for and think about the Power Words as they read.

Guided Practice

Prepare to Read

GENRE STUDY **Fairy tales** are old stories with made-up characters and events that could not happen. As you read *If the Shoe Fits: Two Cinderella Stories*, look for:

- clues that the stories are make-believe
- endings that are happy
- problems and solutions

SET A PURPOSE As you read, **make connections** by finding ways that this text is like things in your life and other texts you have read. This will help you understand and remember the text.

POWER WORDS

- chore
- thrilled
- superb
- beamed
- pleasure
- jealous
- dashed
- hobbled

Meet Pleasant DeSpain.

188

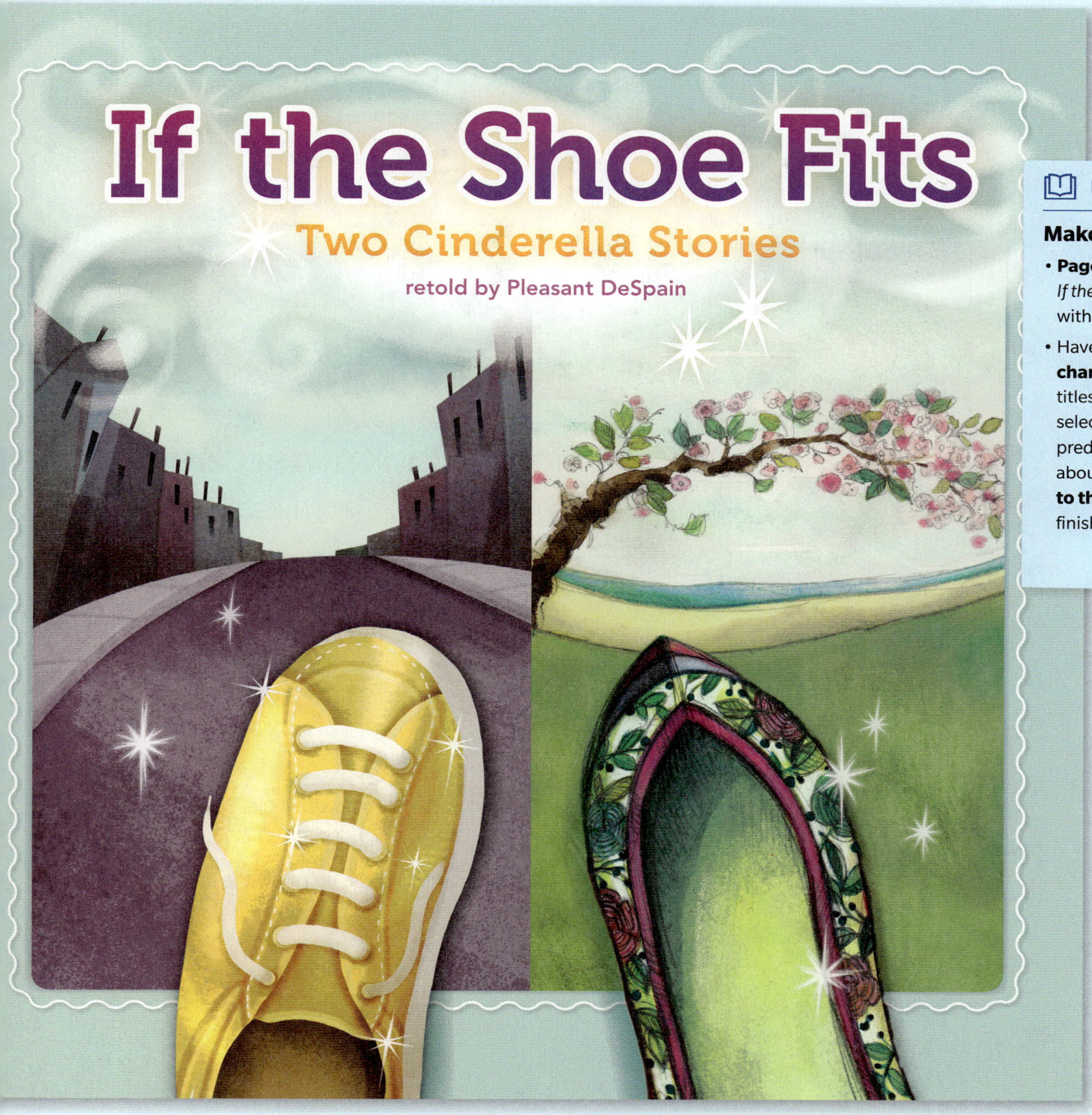

If the Shoe Fits

Two Cinderella Stories

retold by Pleasant DeSpain

 READ FOR UNDERSTANDING

Make Predictions

- **Page through** the beginning of *If the Shoe Fits: Two Cinderella Stories* with children.
- Have them **use prior knowledge, characteristics of the genre,** the titles of the two stories in the selection, and the illustrations to predict what each story will be about. Tell children they will **return to their predictions** after they finish reading the stories.

DOK 2

READ FOR UNDERSTANDING

ASK: Who are the characters in the story? *(Zoey, her stepbrother Finn, her mother)*

ANNOTATION TIP: Have children underline the clue that tells how Finn treats his stepsister, Zoey.

FOLLOW-UP: Who do you think changed the password? Use text evidence to explain. *(Finn changed it. He enjoys playing tricks on Zoey. He laughs when Zoey gets blamed. Zoey looks upset in the illustration and says, "But Mom, I didn't.")*

DOK 3

READ FOR UNDERSTANDING

Make Connections

ASK: Why can't Zoey go to the party? *(Her mother thinks she used the computer without permission.)*

THINK ALOUD *When I was growing up, I remember when my brother blamed me for doing something I did not do. I was very upset because my mother believed my brother and not me. Remembering this helps me understand how Zoey feels about being blamed for changing the password.*

DOK 4

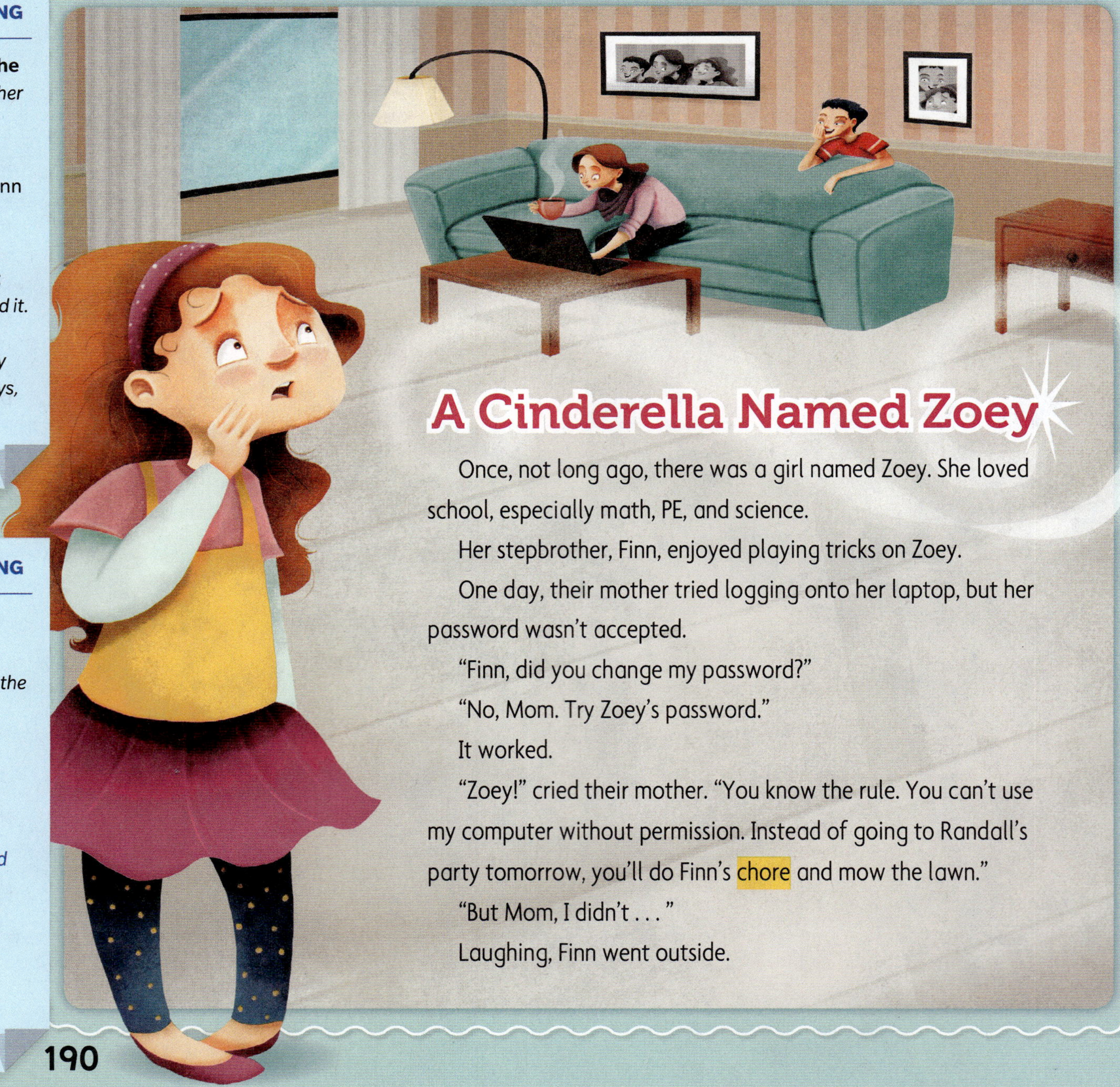

A Cinderella Named Zoey

Once, not long ago, there was a girl named Zoey. She loved school, especially math, PE, and science.

Her stepbrother, Finn, enjoyed playing tricks on Zoey.

One day, their mother tried logging onto her laptop, but her password wasn't accepted.

"Finn, did you change my password?"

"No, Mom. Try Zoey's password."

It worked.

"Zoey!" cried their mother. "You know the rule. You can't use my computer without permission. Instead of going to Randall's party tomorrow, you'll do Finn's chore and mow the lawn."

"But Mom, I didn't . . . "

Laughing, Finn went outside.

190

Randall had invited all his friends to his birthday party. His mom was baking a delicious chocolate cake. He hoped Zoey would come. She was one of his best friends.

The next day, Finn and their mom left for Randall's party.

The doorbell rang. It was Zoey's favorite neighbor, Mrs. Fortuna. She always sparkled!

"Want to go to the party?"

"How did you know?"

"I have a few secrets, dear."

"But the lawn . . ." began Zoey.

Mrs. Fortuna pulled bright red garden shears from her bag. To Zoey's amazement, the shears flew out of Mrs. Fortuna's hands. The lawn was mowed in seconds.

READ FOR UNDERSTANDING

ASK: How do you know you are reading a fairy tale? *(Mrs. Fortuna knows that Zoey can't go to the party. She mows the lawn in seconds using bright red garden shears. The shears fly out of her hands.)*

DOK 2

TARGETED CLOSE READ

Story Structure

Have children reread pages 191–193 to analyze the story's structure.

ASK: What is the conflict Zoey has? *(She wants to go to Randall's party, but she must stay home and do chores.)*

FOLLOW-UP: Summarize how the conflict is resolved and how the story ends. *(Mrs. Fortuna helps her do her chores so she can go to the party. Randall notices Zoey is only wearing one shoe and invites the others to take off a shoe, too.)*

DOK 2

READ FOR UNDERSTANDING

ASK: What happens on the way to the party? *(One of the golden tennis shoes Mrs. Fortuna gave Zoey comes untied and tumbles onto the street and is run over by a bus.)*

FOLLOW-UP: How do Zoey and Mrs. Fortuna feel about what happened? *(Possible response: The illustration shows that they are concerned.)*

DOK 2

READ FOR UNDERSTANDING

Phonics/Decoding in Context

Have children point to the word *Zoey*. Write the word on the board and split the syllables. Remind them that *y* sometimes stands for a vowel sound at the end of a syllable. Explain that in this word, the *y* stands for the long *e* sound. **Guide them to blend** the letters in each syllable and say the word.

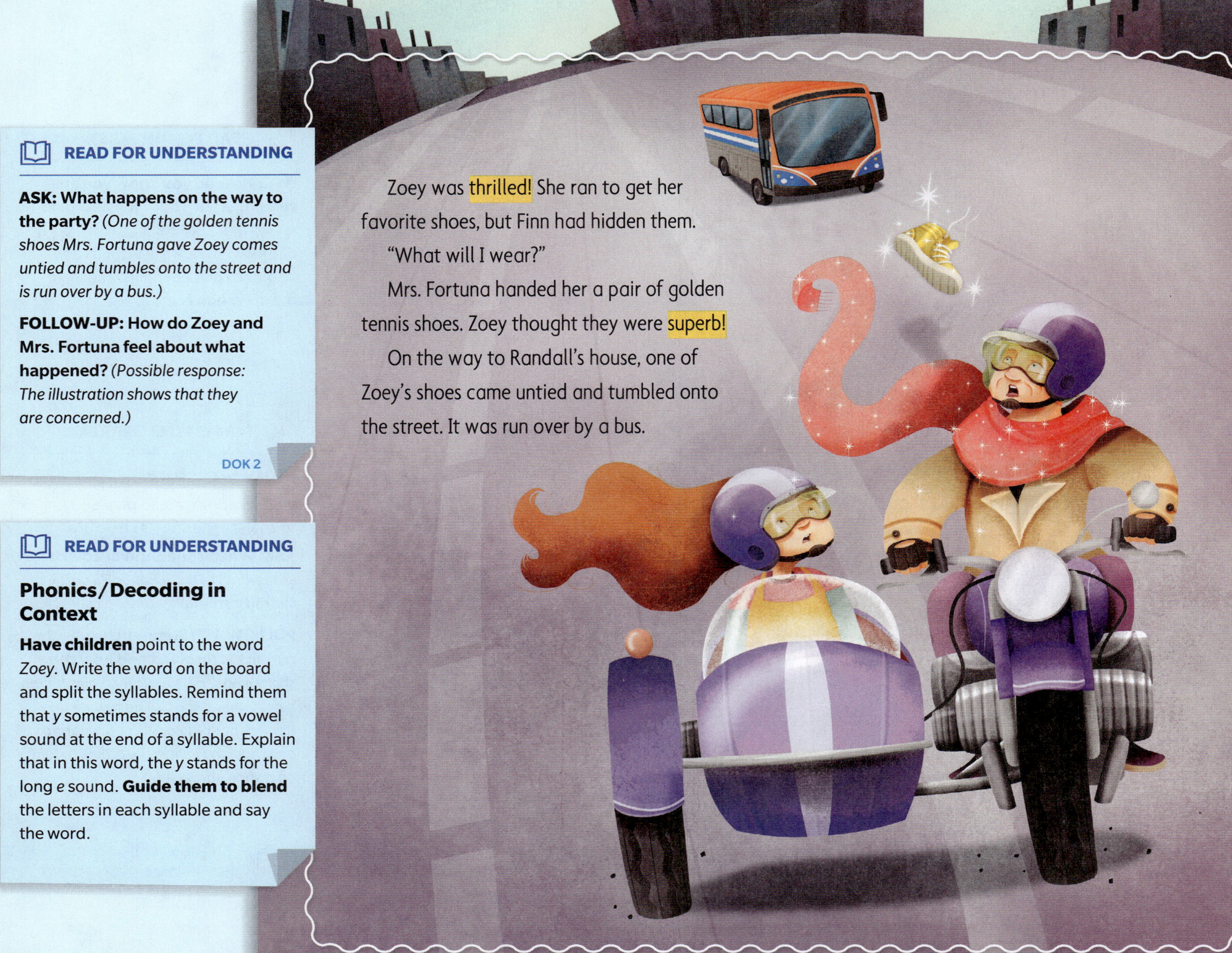

Zoey was thrilled! She ran to get her favorite shoes, but Finn had hidden them.

"What will I wear?"

Mrs. Fortuna handed her a pair of golden tennis shoes. Zoey thought they were superb!

On the way to Randall's house, one of Zoey's shoes came untied and tumbled onto the street. It was run over by a bus.

192

"My shoe!" yelled Zoey.

Mrs. Fortuna consoled her. "Two shoes don't make wishes come true."

Randall beamed when Zoey walked in. He invited her to sit next to him. Noticing her one shoe, he thought, "This is something new." Then he said, "Cool, everyone take off one shoe, just like Zoey."

It was time to cut the cake. The candles were lit, and before Randall blew them out, Zoey smiled. One of her wishes had come true.

193

 **READ FOR UNDERSTANDING**

Quick Teach Words

As needed to support children's comprehension, briefly explain the meaning of *consoled* in this context.

- If you *consoled* someone, you tried to comfort that person because he or she felt sad or disappointed.

 **READ FOR UNDERSTANDING**

Make Connections

MODEL MAKING CONNECTIONS

ASK: How does Randall show that he is a good friend? *(Possible response: He doesn't want Zoey to feel awkward because she is only wearing one shoe. He shows he is a good friend by having everyone take off a shoe.)*

THINK ALOUD *I remember when my friend Howard noticed that I had forgotten my lunch. He gave me half of his sandwich. Good friends watch out for each other.)*

DOK 4

READ FOR UNDERSTANDING

ANNOTATION TIP: Have children label the characters.

FOLLOW-UP: How do Kwan's stepmother and stepsister feel about her? *(They are jealous of Kwan and unkind to her.)* **What details tell you how Kwan feels?** *(Kwan looks very sad in the illustration. She looks unhappy and doesn't feel like she is part of the family.)*

DOK 2

TARGETED CLOSE READ

Story Structure

Have children reread pages 194–198 to analyze the structure of the story.

ASK: Retell the main events of the story. What happens at the beginning? *(Kwan must weed the garden before she can go to the festival.)* **What happens in the middle?** *(A cow eats the weeds and birds give her clothes. She loses a shoe and returns home.)* **What happens at the end?** *(A prince finds her shoe. He discovers it is Kwan's. They live happily ever after.)*

DOK 3

A Cinderella Named Kwan

A Korean Story

Long, long ago, a baby girl was born. Her father named her Kwan, which means "strong."

Sadly, her mother died.

Years later, Kwan's father remarried. His new wife had her own daughter named Hee, which means "pleasure."

Kwan's stepmother and stepsister were jealous of Kwan and unkind to her.

194

One beautiful spring morning, Kwan's stepmother said, "I'm taking Hee to the festival."

"Can I go, honorable mother?" asked Kwan.

"Yes, but first you must weed the garden."

Hee and her mother laughed as they left for the city.

Kwan's heart was heavy. The garden was filled with weeds.

She went outside and was surprised by a large brown cow who said, "I'll eat the weeds."

"Yes, please!" Kwan said.

The cow chomped all the weeds in a flash.

195

 **READ FOR UNDERSTANDING**

Make Connections

ASK: How are Zoey's and Kwan's problems the same? *(Zoey and Kwan are both disappointed because they can't go somewhere.)* **How are they different?** *(Zoey wants to go to a birthday party, but Kwan wants to go to a festival.)*

FOLLOW-UP: What is the same about how each character's chore is done? *(Possible response: Mrs. Fortuna uses shears to mow the lawn in seconds, and a large brown cow chomps all the weeds in a flash.)*

DOK 4

 **READ FOR UNDERSTANDING**

Phonics/Decoding in Context

Have children point to the word *heavy*. Remind them that the vowel team *ea* makes a short *e* sound in some words and a long *e* sound in others. **Model blending the word** using each sound and have children identify which is correct. As time allows, look for other words in the story that contain the vowel team *ea* and have children identify the sound each makes.

 READ FOR UNDERSTANDING

ASK: Does Kwan go to the festival? *(no)* **How do you know? Use details from the story to explain.** *(Kwan loses one of the slippers a flock of songbirds gave her when she trips and falls crossing a river. The slipper goes into the water. She hobbles home instead of going to the festival.)*

DOK 3

 READ FOR UNDERSTANDING

Quick Teach Words

As needed to support children's comprehension, briefly explain the meaning of *flock* in this context.

- A *flock* is a group of birds that travel, rest, or feed together.

Suddenly, a flock of songbirds appeared in the sky, carrying a lovely robe and slippers. "For the strong one," they sang.

Thrilled, Kwan dashed down the road to the bridge crossing the river. She tripped and fell. One of her slippers splashed into the water. "Oh no!" cried Kwan, watching the slipper float away.

Kwan hobbled home and hid the gown and slipper in an old trunk.

196

Meanwhile, a young prince was traveling to the festival. Thirsty, he stopped by the river for a drink. He put his lips into the cold, rushing water, and a beautiful slipper floated by.

"Pretty slipper, pretty lady?" he asked as he grabbed the slipper.

"Pretty lady," sang the birds flying above.

"I must find her," he declared.

197

Notice & Note

Again and Again

- **Remind children** that when an idea or event happens over and over in a story, they should stop to notice and note.
- **Have children** explain why they might use this strategy on pages 196–197. *(Birds help the characters in different ways. They bring Kwan a robe and slippers. They tell the prince that the owner of the slipper is a pretty lady.)*

ANNOTATION TIP: Have children circle the birds in the pictures.

- **Remind them** of the Anchor Question: **Why does the author bring this up again and again?** *(The birds give a clue that something good will happen. That makes me think that the prince who found the slipper will find Kwan.)*

DOK 3

READ FOR UNDERSTANDING

ASK: What happens after the prince arrives at Kwan's farm? *(Hee shoves Kwan to the side and tells the prince the slipper is hers.)*

ANNOTATION TIP: Have children underline how the prince responds to Hee.

FOLLOW-UP: What do the birds tell you about how Kwan's life will change? *(Kwan will be very happy living with the prince.)*

READ FOR UNDERSTANDING

Wrap Up

Revisit the predictions children made before reading. Have them confirm or correct their predictions using evidence from the text and pictures.

DOK 2

The prince traveled to many farms, asking every young woman to try on the slipper. Arriving at Kwan's farm, he showed it to Hee and Kwan.

Hee shoved Kwan to the side, saying, "It's mine!"

"You are not polite," said the prince. "Your sister will try first."

Kwan slipped her foot into the slipper.

"You are strong and beautiful," he said. "Please marry me."

Smiling, Kwan said, "Yes."

The songbirds swirled above. Happy was their song.

198

Respond to Reading

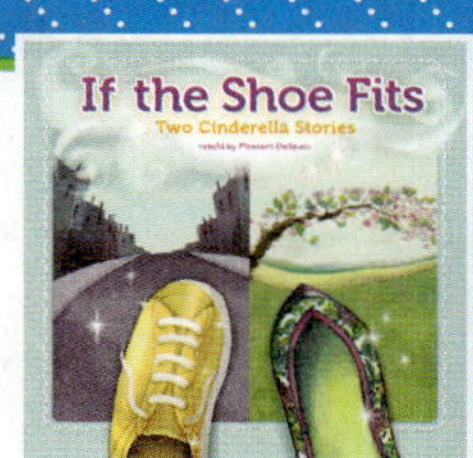

Use details from *If the Shoe Fits: Two Cinderella Stories* to answer these questions with a partner.

1. **Make Connections** How are the two fairy tales alike? What are the most important differences between them?

2. Mrs. Fortuna consoles Zoey when she loses her shoe. Think about a time when you lost something. What made you feel better?

3. If Mrs. Fortuna and the songbirds had not been in the fairy tales, how else could the girls have solved their problems?

Talking Tip

Complete the sentence to add to what your partner says.

My idea is ________.

199

Academic Discussion

Use the TURN AND TALK routine. Remind children to follow agreed-upon rules for discussions, such as listening politely and respectfully and without interrupting as their partner speaks.

Possible responses:

1. *In both stories, a girl wants to go somewhere, she has chores to do, and she gets help from someone. Both stories have magic and a happy ending. One important difference is that the stories are from different cultures. The settings are also different. The Zoey story takes place today and the Kwan story takes place a long time ago. Another important difference is how the story ends. Zoey goes to a party and has fun with her friends. Kwan doesn't go to the festival, but the prince finds her and asks her to marry him.* DOK 4
2. *Answers will vary.* DOK 4
3. *Answers will vary.* DOK 3

Respond to Reading

Write a Comparison

PROMPT Shoes are an important part of both stories. Compare Zoey's shoes with Kwan's shoes. How are their parts in the stories alike? How are they different?

PLAN First, make a list of details about Zoey's shoes. Then, make a list of details about Kwan's shoes. Look for details in the text and illustrations about how they look, where they come from, and what happens to them.

Zoey's shoes	Kwan's shoes

200

Write About Reading

- **Read aloud** the prompt.
- **Lead a discussion** in which children share their ideas about how the characters' shoes are alike and different. Tell them to look for text evidence that describes each pair of shoes and explains what happens to them.
- Then read aloud the Plan section. Have children use ideas from the discussion to help them complete their lists.

DOK 3

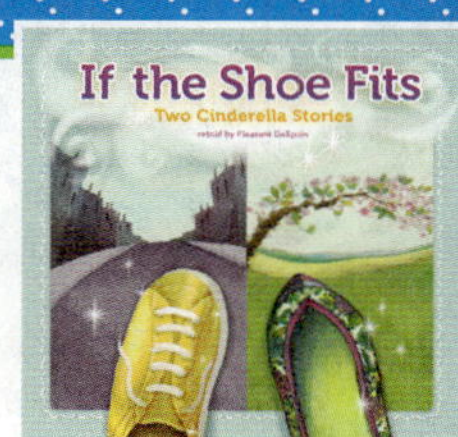

WRITE Now write sentences comparing Zoey's and Kwan's shoes. Use the details in your chart to explain how they are alike and different. Remember to:

- Describe how Zoey and Kwan feel about their shoes.
- Add an apostrophe to show ownership, like *Kwan's shoes*.

Responses will vary.

Write About Reading

- **Read aloud** the Write section.
- **Encourage children** to add descriptive words that help readers understand how Zoey and Kwan feel about their shoes as well as how the shoes are useful to each character.

DOK 3

Independent Close Reading

Have children close read and annotate "The Elves and the Shoemaker" on their own during small-group or independent work time. As needed, **use the Scaffolded Support notes** that follow to guide children who need additional help.

Scaffolded Support

As needed, remind children to:

- make connections to their own life, to the world around them, and to other texts to better understand the characters and plot of the story.
- find details in the text and pictures to help them determine the conflict, or problem, the main character faces and the main events in the plot that lead to a resolution of the problem.

DOK 3

Prepare to Read

GENRE STUDY **Fairy tales** are old stories that have made-up characters and events that could not happen.

MAKE A PREDICTION Preview "The Elves and the Shoemaker." A poor shoemaker needs help. How do you think he will get the help he needs?

The elves might ask the shoemaker if he needs any help.

SET A PURPOSE Read to find out how the shoemaker gets the help he needs.

202

The Elves and the Shoemaker

READ What problem does the shoemaker have? Underline it.

Long ago, there was a kind shoemaker. He worked hard but did not make much money. One night, he went to bed feeling worried. He only had enough material to make one more pair of shoes. He would need to sell them for a good price.

The next morning, the shoemaker was amazed. In his workshop, he found the prettiest shoes he had ever seen! He sold them for a very good price. With the money, he bought material to make two more pairs of shoes.

The shoemaker felt grateful. He felt curious, too. Who was his mystery helper?

Close Reading Tip

Number the main events on this page in order.

Scaffolded Support

As needed remind children that:

- a story's problem, or conflict, is often explained at the beginning of the story.
- numbering the plot events as they read can help them identify the story's main events and understand how they lead to a resolution.

DOK 2

READ How is the shoemaker's problem solved?

That night, he went to bed feeling happy. The next morning, he was amazed again! He found two beautiful pairs of shoes that he sold for a very, very good price.

This happened night after night. The shoemaker wanted to thank his helper. One night he stayed up late. To his surprise, three little barefoot elves entered his workshop and got right to work. The next night, the elves got a surprise. The shoemaker had made tiny pairs of boots just for them!

To thank the shoemaker, the elves showed him how to make fancy shoes. The shoemaker was never poor again.

Close Reading Tip

Write a **C** when you make a connection to an event in your life.

Scaffolded Support

As needed, remind children to:

- pay attention to events that are repeated and think about why they might be important enough to happen over and over. What might they reveal about the characters?
- think about how experiences they've had are similar to ones described in the story in order to better understand how the characters are feeling and why they act the way they do.

DOK 4

CHECK MY UNDERSTANDING

Which events are repeated? How are those events an important part of the story?

The elves help the shoemaker night after night. That is how the shoemaker's problem is solved.

Cite Text Evidence

WRITE ABOUT IT Compare "The Elves and the Shoemaker" to the Cinderella stories. How is kindness an important part of each story? Use details about the characters to support your answer.

Kindness is an important part of each story because the elves, Mrs. Fortuna, and the songbirds do something kind for others.

Scaffolded Support

As needed, guide children to think about the different acts of kindness performed in each story and use this information to infer what the characters in each text are like.

DOK 4

Guided Practice

 **VIEW FOR UNDERSTANDING**

Introduce the Video

- **Read aloud** and discuss the information about the genre.
- **Guide children** to set a purpose for viewing to identify the cause and effect relationships presented in the video.
- **Provide** information about the background topic, crows.

Prepare to View

GENRE STUDY **Videos** are short movies that give you information or something for you to watch for enjoyment. As you watch *Those Clever Crows*, notice:

- how pictures, sounds, and words work together
- what the video is about
- information about the topic
- the tone or mood of the video

SET A PURPOSE Ask yourself what happens and why to make **cause and effect** connections about the video. A cause is something that makes something else happen. An effect is what happens because of the cause.

Build Background: Crows

206

THOSE CLEVER CROWS

from *The New York Times*

VIEW FOR UNDERSTANDING

Make Predictions

- **Display** the title page of *Those Clever Crows* for children.
- Have them **use prior knowledge** and the cover to predict what the video will be about. Tell children they will **return to their predictions** after they finish watching the video.

DOK 2

VIEW FOR UNDERSTANDING

Cause and Effect

ASK: What cause and effect did the crows learn by doing the experiment? *(They learned that dropping certain objects into the tube would make the food rise so that they could reach it.)*

FOLLOW-UP: What did the scientists learn about the crows by covering up parts of the tube? *(They learned that the crows could not understand the cause and effect unless they could see it happening.)*

DOK 2

VIEW FOR UNDERSTANDING

Wrap Up

Revisit the predictions children made before viewing. Have them confirm or correct their predictions using evidence from the video.

DOK 2

As You View Are crows clever? You decide! Watch the crows' behavior. Think carefully about how the words help you understand what the crows are doing. What do you think those crows must be thinking?

208

Respond to Media

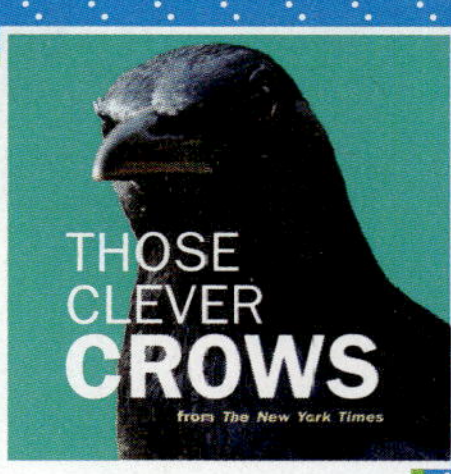

Use details from *Those Clever Crows* to answer these questions with a partner.

1. **Cause and Effect** What do the crows want to make happen? How do their actions help them reach their goal?

2. How are the crows in the video like the crows in the fable? How are they different?

3. Do you think *Those Clever Crows* is a good title for this video? Use details from the video to explain your ideas.

Talking Tip

Wait for your turn to speak. Talk about your feelings and ideas clearly.

I feel that ________.

Academic Discussion

Use the TURN AND TALK routine. Remind children to follow agreed-upon rules for discussions, such as making sure they use words that clearly describe their feelings and ideas when it is their turn to speak.

Possible responses:

1. *They want to make the food rise high enough for them to reach it. They keep putting objects in the tube that make the food rise.* DOK 2
2. *The crows in the fable and the video both drop objects into water to help them reach something. The crows in the fable are characters who can talk. The crows in the video are real crows.* DOK 3
3. *Answers will vary.* DOK 2

Module Wrap-Up

Let's Wrap Up!

Essential Question

What lessons can we learn from the characters in stories?

Pick one of these activities to show what you have learned about the topic.

1. Learn Your Lesson

Think of a lesson that kids can use in their everyday lives. Then write your own fable or fairy tale that teaches that lesson. Look back at the texts for ideas. See how many of those characters you can include in your new story!

210

Revisit the Essential Question

- **Read aloud** the Essential Question.
- **Remind children** that in this module, they read different texts about storytelling that can help them answer the question.
- **Have children** choose one of the activities to show what they learned in this module.

Learn Your Lesson

- **Guide children** to think about a lesson they might find helpful in their own lives. Have them ask themselves: How could this lesson help me? How would it help make my daily life better? How might it help other kids like me?
- **Encourage children** to use the Big Idea Word *moral* in their stories.

DOK 3

2. Story Catalog

Make a catalog of things fables or fairy tales need. Look back at the texts for ideas. Then draw pictures of characters, settings, or objects you might find in those kinds of stories. Label each picture.

Word Challenge

Can you use the word moral in your catalog?

Story Catalog

- **Guide children** to use a concept map or web to begin organizing their ideas. They can put one story element (for example, *Characters*) in the center circle and list examples or descriptions of that element (for example, *princess, magical*) in the surrounding circles.
- **Gather children's ideas** into one master catalog that can be used by the class as a writing reference.

DOK 3

My Notes

Brainstorm and Plan

Have children use the My Notes space to jot down ideas for their chosen activity. Remind them to refer back to their notes as they complete the activity.

Glossary

A

argue [är′gyo͞o] When you **argue**, you speak in an angry way that shows you do not agree.
Do not **argue** with your brother.

B

beamed

beamed [bēmd] Someone who **beamed** gave a big smile.
Caleb **beamed** when he read the funny story.

believe [bĭ-lēv′] When you **believe** something, you think it is true.
I **believe** that it will rain today.

bind

bind [bīnd] When you **bind** something, you tie it up.
He will **bind** the books together with string.

blamed [blāmd] When you are **blamed**, someone thinks you did something wrong.
The kids **blamed** each other for the mess.

212

booming [bo͞om′ĭng] Something that is **booming** is loud like thunder.

The **booming** sounds let us know that the fireworks show had started.

booming

C

chore [chôr] A **chore** is a job you must do.

His **chore** is to take out the trash.

chore

clever [klĕv′ər] Someone who is **clever** is very smart.

My dog is **clever** and knows many tricks.

clue [klo͞o] A **clue** is information that helps you find an answer.

The open door was a **clue** that the lock needed to be fixed.

compromise [kŏm′prə-mīz′] A **compromise** is when people agree to something by each giving up a little of what they want.

The team agreed on a **compromise**.

213

cozy

decision

cozy [kō'zē] A place that is **cozy** is comfortable.
The fireplace made the room very **cozy**.

D

dashed [dăsht] If you **dashed**, you ran quickly.
My dad **dashed** out the door to get to work on time.

decision [dĭ-sĭzh'ən] When you make a **decision**, you make up your mind about something.
I will make a **decision** about what to have for a snack.

disagreement [dĭs'ə-grē'mənt] In a **disagreement**, people have different ideas about things.
They had a **disagreement** about what game to play.

disturb [dĭ-stûrb'] When you **disturb** someone, you bother that person.
Please do not **disturb** me while I'm sleeping.

dragged [drăgd] If you **dragged** something, you worked hard to pull it along the ground.
The boy **dragged** the heavy suitcase across the floor.

214

E

excuses [ĭk-skyo͞os′ĭz] **Excuses** are reasons why you cannot do something.
He tried to make **excuses** for breaking the pitcher, but then he just apologized.

excuses

F

frown [froun] A **frown** is a sad or angry look.
The boy had a **frown** on his face.

fulfill [fo͝ol-fĭl′] When you **fulfill** something, you make it happen.
I always **fulfill** a promise.

G

greedy [grē′dē] Someone who is **greedy** wants more than what is fair.
Todd was being **greedy** with the popcorn.

greedy

hesitant

H

hesitant [hĕz′ĭ-tənt] If you are **hesitant**, you do something slowly because you are not sure about it.
At first, Dan was **hesitant** to try the salad.

hobbled [hŏb′əld] If you **hobbled**, you walked in a slow, uneven way.
The boy **hobbled** home after he hurt his leg.

invited

I

invited [ĭn-vīt′ĭd] When you are **invited** to a party, you have been asked to come.
My big brother **invited** me to go to the talent show with him and his friends.

J

jealous [jĕl′əs] If you are **jealous**, you feel angry because you want what someone else has.
I felt **jealous** when Emma won first place.

216

journey [jûr′nē] A **journey** is a trip from one place to another.
The map helped Cheri plan her **journey**.

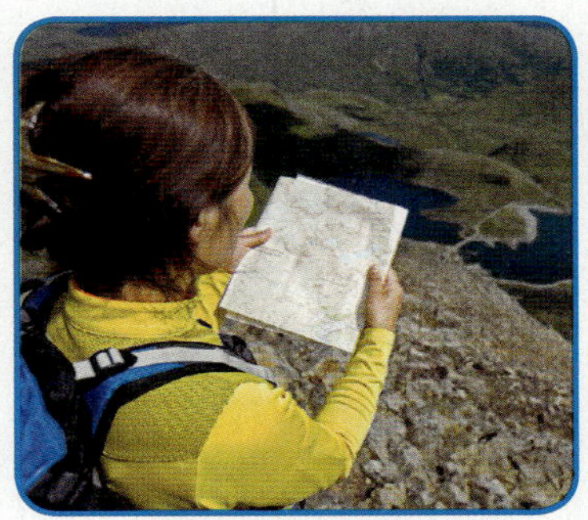
journey

M

moral [môr′əl, mŏr′əl] A **moral** is a lesson in a story.
The **moral** of the story is to keep trying.

mumbled [mŭm′bəld] If you **mumbled**, you spoke quietly and not very clearly.
She **mumbled** something that I did not understand.

musical [myōō′zĭ-kəl] Something that is **musical** has a tune.
A trumpet is a **musical** instrument.

N

narrow [năr′ō] Something that is **narrow** is thin and has little space.
It was hard for cars and bikes to fit together on the very **narrow** street.

narrow

nearby [nîr′bī′] Someone who is **nearby** is close to where you are.
My friend lives in a **nearby** house.

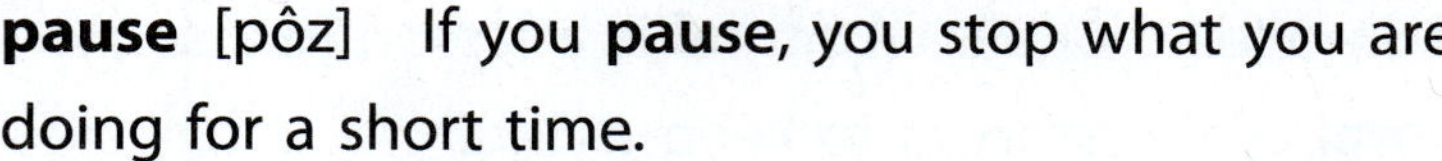

pause [pôz] If you **pause**, you stop what you are doing for a short time.
The speaker will **pause** so we can ask questions.

persuade [pər-swād′] When you **persuade**, you try to get others to feel or think as you do.
Please **persuade** her to join the fun.

plain

plain [plān] A **plain** is a flat piece of land with few trees.
We saw beautiful flowers on the **plain**.

plead

plead [plēd] When you **plead**, you ask someone in a strong, hopeful way.
We **plead** with our mother to let us go to the party.

218

pleasure [plĕzh'ər] **Pleasure** is a feeling of happiness or joy.
It is always a **pleasure** to see you.

practice [prăk'tĭs] **Practice** is when you do something over and over to get better at it.
I try to **practice** piano every day.

practice

R

rattled [răt'ld] Something that **rattled** made many short, shaking noises.
The coins **rattled** in my pocket.

relate [rĭ-lāt'] If you **relate** to someone, you know how the person feels.
I can **relate** to how the character in this story is feeling.

respectful [rĭ-spĕkt'fəl] **Respectful** words are words that are polite and kind.
The players are **respectful** of each other.

respectful

219

S

scoots [sko͞ots] When someone **scoots**, he or she moves very quickly.
He **scoots** out the door so he won't miss the bus.

screams

screams [skrēmz] When someone **screams**, he or she yells loudly.
She **screams** with excitement on her favorite ride in the amusement park.

scurries [skûr′ēz, skŭr′ēz] When someone **scurries**, he or she moves with short, fast steps.
The chipmunk **scurries** across the yard.

sense [sĕns] Something that makes **sense** is easy to understand.
It makes **sense** to practice before the big game.

shove

shove [shŭv] When you **shove** something, you push it hard.
Ian will **shove** the wagon for his sister.

skill [skĭl] If you have great **skill** at something, you do that thing really well.
Ethel can bake with great **skill**, and she loves to share with her friends.

speech [spēch] A **speech** is a talk you give to an audience.
My friend gave an inspiring **speech** after she won an award for her good citizenship.

steaming [stēm'ĭng] If something is **steaming**, it is very hot.
The soup was **steaming**, so we had to wait a few minutes for it to cool.

superb [so͞o-pûrb'] Something that is **superb** is the very best.
The celebration we had for my grandfather's birthday was **superb**!

skill

steaming

tackled

thrilled

T

tackled [tăk′əld] If you **tackled** someone, you pushed the person to the ground.
He **tackled** the player with the football.

threatening [thrĕt′n-ĭng] People who are **threatening** to do something are warning they will do it.
The group is **threatening** to quit if they don't get their own way.

thrilled [thrĭld] When you are **thrilled**, you are very excited.
The kids were **thrilled** to go camping.

V

version [vûr′zhən] A **version** is a different or changed form of something.
We played a new **version** of the game.

222

W

wrinkled [rĭng'kəld] You **wrinkled** up your face if you tightened muscles to make folds and lines in your skin.
The baby **wrinkled** his little forehead.

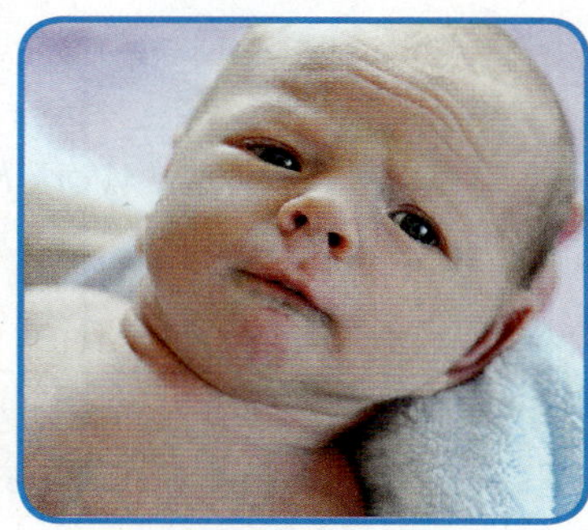

wrinkled

Y

yanked [yăngkd] If you **yanked** something, you pulled it hard and fast.
The whole team **yanked** on the rope during the game of tug of war.

223

Index of Titles and Authors

224

Acknowledgments

Big Red Lollipop by Rukhsana Khan. Illustrated by Sophie Blackall. Text copyright © 2010 by Rukhsana Khan. Illustrations copyright © 2010 by Sophie Blackall. Reprinted by permission of Viking Children's Books, an imprint of Penguin Young Readers Group, a division of Penguin Random House LLC and Charlotte Sheedy Literary Agency.

Gingerbread for Liberty! (retitled from *Gingerbread for Liberty!: How a German Baker Helped Win the American Revolution*) by Mara Rockliff, illustrated by Vincent X. Kirsch. Text copyright © 2015 by Mara Rockliff. Illustrations copyright © 2015 by Vincent X. Kirsch. Reprinted by permission of Houghton Mifflin Harcourt Publishing Company and the Andrea Brown Literary Agency.

How to Read a Story by Kate Messner. Illustrated by Mark Siegel. Text copyright © 2015 by Kate Messner. Illustrations copyright © 2015 by Mark Siegel. Reprinted by permission of Chronicle Books LLC.

Pepita and the Bully/Pepita y la peleonera by Ofelia Dumas Lachtman, illustrated by Alex Pardo DeLange. Spanish translation by Gabriela Baeza Ventura. Text copyright © 2011 by Ofelia Dumas Lachtman. Illustrations copyright © 2011 by Alex Pardo DeLange. Reprinted by permission of Arte Público Press - University of Houston.

Excerpt from *Working with Others* by Robin Nelson. Text copyright © 2006 by Lerner Publishing Group, Inc. Reprinted with the permission of Lerner Publications Company, a division of Lerner Publishing Group, Inc.

Credits

4 (b) ©Rawpixel.com/Shutterstock; 7 (b) ©Voropaeva/Shutterstock; 8 ©GagliardiImages/Shutterstock, ©giedre vaitekune/Shutterstock, ©Suriya Phosri/iStock/Getty Images Plus/Getty Images; ©BraunS/E+/Getty Images; 12 ©Miloje/Shutterstock; 13 ©Miloje/Shutterstock; 14 ©Penguin Group; 40 ©Rawpixel.com/Shutterstock; 41 ©Rawpixel.com/Shutterstock; 42 ©kali9/E+/Getty Images; 43 ©Amble Design/Shutterstock; 44 (l) ©Hero Images/Getty Images; 44 (r) ©Leila Mendez/Cultura/Getty Images; 45 ©Paul Viant/The Image Bank/Getty Images; 46 ©szefei/Shutterstock; 47 ©asiseeit/E+/Getty Images; 48 ©Sergey Novikov/Shutterstock; 49 ©Milica Nistoran/Shutterstock; 50 ©ImagesBazaar/Getty Images; 51 (tr) ©Rawpixel.com/Shutterstock; 53 (tr) ©Rawpixel.com/Shutterstock; 54 (l) ©Duplass/Shutterstock; 54 (r) ©YiorgosGR/iStock/Getty Images Plus/Getty Images; 55 (l) ©ND1939/iStock/Getty Images Plus/Getty Images; 55 (c) ©baona/iStock/Getty Images Plus/Getty Images; 55 (r) ©LydiaGoolia/iStock/Getty Images Plus; 56 ©baona/iStock/Getty Images Plus/Getty Images; 58 Courtesy of Houghton Mifflin Harcourt; 80 ©SZ Photo/Scherl/Sueddeutsche Zeitung Photo/Alamy; 82 ©Franklin D. Roosevelt Presidential Library & Museum; 84 ©2011 Arte Público Press - University of Houston; 110 ©Monkey Business Images/Shutterstock; 118 ©Monkey Business Images/Shutterstock; 119 ©Wavebreakmedia/iStock/Getty Images Plus/Getty Images; 126 ©HMH/Andy Duback; 152 ©Crystal Hubbard; 166 ©holbox/Shutterstock; 188 ©Sidney Fleisher; 206 ©Steve Byland/iStockPhoto.com; 207 ©Voropaeva/Shutterstock; 208 (b) ©PARS International Corp; 209 (tr) ©Voropaeva/Shutterstock; 210 ©fotostorm/iStock/Getty Images Plus; 210 (inset) ©Art'nLera/Shutterstock; 211 (inset) ©Art'nLera/Shutterstock; 211 ©OlScher/Shutterstock; 212 (b) ©irene_k/Shutterstock; 212 (t) ©Daniel Laflor/The Agency Collection/Getty Images; 213 (b) ©TinnaPong/Shutterstock; 213 (t) ©Photodisc/Getty Images; 214 (t) ©Corbis; 214 (b) ©Julia Kuznetsova/Shutterstock; 215 (b) ©Serhii Bobyk/Shutterstock; 215 (t) ©Houghton Mifflin Harcourt; 216 (t) ©michaeljung/Shutterstock; 216 (b) ©Asier Romero/Shutterstock; 217 (b) ©Bumble Dee/Shutterstock; 217 (t) ©Henn Photography/Cultura/Corbis; 218 (t) ©djgis/Shutterstock; 218 (b) ©EduardSV/Shutterstock; 219 (b) ©Houghton Mifflin Harcourt; 219 (t) ©Picturenet/Blend Images/Getty Images; 220 (t) ©Purestock/Getty Images; 220 (b) ©Ilene MacDonald/Alamy Images; 221 (t) ©Kei Shooting/Shutterstock; 221 (b) ©Lesterman/Shutterstock; 222 (b) ©Daniel Pangbourne/Digital Vision/Getty Images; 222 (t) ©Orange Line Media/Shutterstock; 223 ©Elena Stepanova/Shutterstock